BBC BOOKS

LETTER TO DANIEL

Fergal Keane OBE is one of the BBC's most distinguished correspondents, having worked for the corporation in Northern Ireland, South Africa, Asia and the Balkans. He has been awarded a BAFTA and has been named reporter of the year on television and radio, winning honours from the Royal Television Society and the Sony Radio Awards. He has also been named Reporter of the Year in the Amnesty International Press Awards and won the James Cameron Prize and the Edward R. Murrow Award from the US Overseas Press Association. His other books include *The Bondage of Fear*, *Season of Blood* (winner of the 1995 Orwell Prize), *Letter to Daniel* and *Letters Home*. All of these titles are available in Penguin.

Fergal Keane was born in London and educated in Ireland, where he keeps a small cottage on the south-east coast.

LETTER TO DANIEL

Despatches from the Heart

Fergal Keane

EDITED BY
Tony Grant

BBC BOOKS
PENGUIN BOOKS

PENGUIN BOOKS
BBC BOOKS
Published by the Penguin Group
Penguin Books Ltd, 27 Wrights Lane, London W8 5TZ, England
Penguin Putnam Inc., 375 Hudson Street, New York, New York 10014, USA
Penguin Books Australia Ltd, Ringwood, Australia
Penguin Books Canada Ltd, 10 Alcorn Avenue, Toronto, Ontario, Canada, M4V 3B2
Penguin Books (NZ) Ltd, 182–190 Walrau Road, Auckland 10, New Zealand
Penguin Books Ltd, Registered Offices: Harmondsworth, Middlesex, England

First published 1996
22
© Fergal Keane, 1996
The moral right of the author has been asserted
🄱🄱🄒 ™ BBC used under licence
Set in Joanna MT
Printed and bound in Great Britain by Clays Ltd, St Ives plc

All pieces originally written for BBC Radio 4's From Our Own Correspondent except 'My
Grandmother's House' and 'Local Lessons' (not previously broadcast or published); 'A
Correspondent's Diary', 'Map-makers of Apartheid', 'The Chicken Farm', 'The Nature
of Racism' and 'Poem for John' (BBC Worldwide Magazine); 'Letter to my Father',
'Sound of the City' and 'Father Joe's Outing' (BBC Radio 4 Four Corners); 'The
Indispensable Afrikaner' (The Spectator); 'The Land of the Dead' and 'Season of Blood'
(Penguin Books); 'Spiritual Damage' (The Guardian); 'Farewell Hong Kong' (Aer Lingus'
Cara magazine); 'St Patrick's Day in Taipei' (BBC Radio 4 Afternoon Shift); 'The Lady and
the Generals' (You magazine); 'No Man is an Island' (BBC Radio 4 series).

'It is with the heart one sees rightly;
what is essential is invisible to the eye.'
ANTOINE DE ST EXUPERY

CONTENTS

Part Three: Asia

Part Four: No Man is an Island

For Eamon Patrick Keane, d. 5 January 1990 and
his grandson, Daniel Patrick Keane, b. 4 February 1996

AUTHOR'S FOREWORD

One week before the birth of our first child, Daniel, the editor of *From Our Own Correspondent* (FOOC) for BBC Radio 4, Tony Grant, rang and suggested I write a piece about becoming a father. At first, I was reluctant to go ahead. My own childhood had been troubled and I would not have been able to write honestly without some reference to the past. Allied to that is the difficult question of just how much of him/herself a foreign correspondent can legitimately inject into what they write, even for a programme with as broad a remit as FOOC. I have always tried to write from the heart as well as the head and knew that a despatch about fatherhood would have to be a deeply personal exercise. That would leave me open to criticism from those inside and outside the BBC who feel that such a personal style has no place in the world of news and current affairs.

But then, on a wonderful night in early February, Daniel arrived and I found myself caught in the grip of emotions I could never have foreseen. I knew I simply had to write what I was seeing and remembering. The subsequent 'Letter to Daniel', which I wrote for FOOC, spoke of my memories of children and war and of my own beginnings some thirty-five years earlier. Within minutes of the broadcast ending the FOOC office was inundated with calls requesting transcripts and copies of the tape.

In the days, weeks and months that followed I received hundreds of letters from people who had heard the broadcast and wanted to share their feelings. Many were people who had experienced deep personal loss in their own lives or who had recently become parents. The Letter clearly touched a chord not only in Britain but among the vast audiences of the BBC World Service which broadcast it a week later.

Several newspapers, including the *Daily Mail* and the *Independent*, reprinted the Letter, and this led to a further round of correspondence. Many of the letters asked if my BBC writings had been collected and if they were available in print. Although I have written two books, one on South Africa, *The Bondage of Fear*, the other on Rwanda, *Season of Blood*, there is no collection of the pieces I have written for FOOC and numerous newspapers and magazines.

This book aims to bring together my own favourite pieces from the past six years of my work with the BBC. It draws on my travels in Africa and Asia and on topics as diverse as my grandmother's house and my first weeks as a trainee local reporter. My eternal gratitude is due to my editor, Tony Grant, and his wonderful assistant, Judith Hart, for their efforts in compiling this book.

This work stands separate from the daily work of news reporting and analysis which takes up the vast majority of time as a BBC correspondent. It reflects, as the title suggests, a more personal engagement with the stories and people I encountered over the past six years. I believe passionately in a journalism that speaks from the heart and the mind, and FOOC, that most wonderful of all BBC programmes, is the perfect vehicle for this.

I am talking about simply trying to tell them what it is like to stand where I do, and see the things I see. Sometimes these things fill me with horror, at other times they light up my senses. Because I have reported on some of the more terrible events of the late twentieth century there is in parts of this book a somewhat apocalyptic tone. This is particularly true of the Rwandan genocide which left me with questions about humanity I doubt I will ever be able to answer.

And yet, for all that, I hope there is in these pages an ultimate sense of glad engagement with the world, a pulsing curiosity which sends me out each day to explore, not in fear but in hope.

Fergal Keane

Part One

IRELAND, FAMILY AND FRIENDS

MY GRANDMOTHER'S HOUSE

Cork, May 1996

Happy childhood summers were spent at grandmother's ivy-covered house in the hills near the city of Cork in south-west Ireland.

When they first came to Turners Cross my grandparents could see fields stretching for miles from their sitting-room window. It was still 'the country' back then. My mother remembers that there were farms nearby where people raised cattle and spoke with broad accents quite different from the lilting cadences of the city. Beyond the pasturelands was a range of hills which formed the last barrier before the land levelled down to the Atlantic Ocean and the coastal towns of Kinsale and Crosshaven. In winter when the offshore winds swept in around the Old Head of Kinsale, the people of the new suburb could smell brine on the air.

On the other side of Turners Cross, down in the valley, sat the city of Cork built around the mouth of the River Lee on a series of islands. These were joined together by numerous bridges and above them rose the steeples of many churches like a vast and elegant ocean liner. On summer days the entire population seemed drawn to the river, floating on boats or sauntering along its banks in the shade of tall trees. It was a favourite place for lovers and on summer nights their long whisperings floated among the branches and out over the currents. But in winter when floods rose the same people who had walked, fished, swum and loved in summer would curse their proximity to the water.

Thus my grandfather was careful to pick a spot high above the city where there was no chance of flooding. The northern

13

hills of Cork had long ago been settled. Here the merchants who had made their fortune exporting butter to the Continent had built great mansions in imitation of the splendid villas of Italy where they holidayed each year. My grandfather built his house, St Declans, on the southern hills seven years before the outbreak of the Second World War. In those days Turners Cross was a place of stillness and quiet. Only later in the boom years of the late forties and fifties would it succumb to the designs of the city planners. Then avenue after avenue sprang up until the green fields had disappeared under a carpet of concrete.

My grandfather's name was Paddy Hassett and he married my grandmother, May Sexton, in the summer of 1932. The house he built for his new bride sat in its own garden with a rockery full of flowers, several apple trees and numerous blackcurrant bushes. It was made of solid west Cork stone and, in the first year of their occupation, they planted ivy which soon spread across the walls. Every few months this had to be sheared back lest it sneak across the windows and block out the sunlight.

Like many Irish couples of the time my grandparents had a large family. There were eight children in all, of whom seven lived beyond childhood. I believe the decision to have a large family was based less on any deep religious conviction than from a profound love of life. They were devout Catholics, but their sense of humour and warmth kept at bay the more puritanical and narrow notions which infected the lives of so many people in the Ireland of that time.

My grandfather died when I was one year old and what I know of him has been gleaned from the stories of my family. I know that he was a quiet man who neither smoked nor drank. But he had a romantic nature and loved opera and the Irish game of hurling. More than anything he loved his children. Once a week he and my grandmother would go into town for tea and afterwards to the cinema. It was, as far as I know, the only time in the week which was not devoted to the interests and well-being of their growing brood of children.

My grandfather ran his own garage business and made a good income in the postwar years when cars began to appear for the first time on Ireland's narrow roads. He built a seaside cottage for his family near the village of Ardmore in County Waterford where he had been born, the son of a police sergeant. Every June my grandmother would load her family on to the bus and set off for the cottage where they stayed until the end of August. But it was the house at Turners Cross which remained at the centre of the family. My mother remembers it as a place crowded with children's voices and music.

Then in the early sixties my grandfather's business collapsed, a victim of recession and his own unending willingness to give credit to those who would never repay him. For a while it looked as if the bank would take the house, but then my grandfather's eldest son stepped in and took out a mortgage on the property.

He died a few months later from the effects of a stroke. I know that, close to the end, my grandmother brought me, their first grandchild, to see him in hospital and that he stroked my infant head. He wanted to speak but could not and he never left hospital. My grandmother returned alone to the house they had built on the hills above the river.

In retrospect, much of my grandmother's later life seems to have been a hard struggle for emotional survival. She had already suffered the loss of her husband and the death of a child shortly after birth. Then she lost a fourteen-year-old son, Ben, to polio. But it was the death of her third son, Michael, in a fire in New York City, which came close to destroying her faith in life. Michael had been a favourite. A talented theatre director, he had emigrated to America in the 1950s but was weeks away from returning to Ireland when a fire in his apartment claimed his life. Warm-hearted, artistic and handsome, he closely resembled my grandfather. The mention of his name would bring tears to my grandmother's eyes until the day she died.

And yet, in spite of her immense sorrow, May Hassett kept going. She still managed to smile and make us laugh. Although I suspect her own hope disappeared on the night Michael died, she communicated her love for others with such power that those around her always felt happy and wanted. I spent most of my childhood summers living with her in St Declans. My memories are of a happy place where comfort and reassurance were always at hand. Because of my father's alcoholism, my own home environment was neither happy nor secure. Taking the train to Cork and St Declans and the warm arms of my grandmother seemed to me an annual deliverance.

When my parents separated permanently in 1970, I went to live in St Declans for two years. It was a traumatic time, a time of great upheaval, and I would almost certainly have become lost in bad places had the lights of my grandparents' house not beckoned. I remember many things about that house: the smell of brown bread baking in the kitchen, collecting armfuls of apples in the garden for crab apple jelly, picking blackcurrants for jam, playing endless games of 'kiss or torture' with my friends' sisters, choking desperately on my first cigarette in the shed at the end of the garden while my grandmother laughed to herself in the kitchen.

On rainy afternoons my grandmother would bring down the big box of toy soldiers collected over the years by her own sons and I would lose myself in imaginary battles and conquests. Later, when I saw a girl I wanted to ask out, it was my grandmother who gave me the courage to venture forth, a teenage Romeo in brushed denim jeans, and suggest a trip to the cinema. 'The worst she can say is no,' she told me and, as always, she was right. In fact the girl said 'Yes,' and our relationship lasted, believe it or not, for eight years. When we broke up and I was plunged into extended youthful misery my grandmother was waiting in St Declans with a mug of cocoa and a sympathetic smile.

I left Cork and the world of my childhood in 1979 and began a journalistic career that would take me to places my grandparents had barely heard of. As the years went on, I saw less and less of my grandmother. Yet each time I came back to St Declans she seemed to be the strong warm person I had always known. And then, while living in Belfast, I received news that she was suffering from cancer. When I went to see her she seemed frail and suddenly old, and she told me she believed she was dying. 'I'm on the way out Ferg,' she said and then added, 'but we all have to go some time.'

That evening I went up to St Declans and the house felt empty and strange. There were no voices now. Only her photographs on the walls, some of them fading into yellow, spoke of its crowded past. My grandmother was eventually transferred to the Royal Marsden Hospital in London where the doctors seemed more optimistic. At about the same time I was appointed BBC correspondent in South Africa, a job I had wanted from the moment I joined the Corporation. My grandmother was delighted for me and even spoke hopefully of being there to greet me at St Declans when I came home in the summer.

On our way out to South Africa my wife and I stopped off in London to visit her at the Royal Marsden. There, among other old people, in a city she did not know, my grandmother seemed small and vulnerable, a little old lady for whom unseen shadows were lengthening every day. We spoke about the past and about our large group of relatives, and she told me to take care of myself and my wife, Anne. 'Mind that little girl,' she joked.

When I got up to go I noticed that my grandmother had tears in her eyes and we both knew, without saying a word, that I would never see her again. She took my hand in hers and whispered into my ear, 'Always remember, love, that I will be watching out for you, wherever you are, always.'

A month later she came home to die. I was given the news early one morning on a long-distance call from Ireland. I walked out into the garden and cried for a long time. And then, with the birds of the highveld singing their hearts out, I went back inside and woke my wife. We sat for hours drinking tea and remembering my grandmother, and I am happy to say that most of the memories involved laughter. After her death my uncle decided to sell St Declans and the rest of the family agreed. There seemed little point in clinging to bricks and mortar when the people we had loved, who had made the place special, had passed on.

Yet each summer when I return to Cork I cannot resist the urge to drive past St Declans. I always stop there for a few moments and lean back into warm invisible arms, imagining that I can hear the sound of opera playing on the radio and children's voices rising above it, and then a woman calling them home for tea. Home as it always will be.

LOCAL LESSONS

Limerick, June 1996

The author began his career in journalism with a reporter's job on a newspaper in the midwest of Ireland.

I had just reached the top of the stairs when the voice from the kitchen called up. 'Mister, what time will you be wanting your dinner?' Mister? Somebody was calling me Mister! I was a few months short of nineteen and somebody was, for the first time in my life, calling me Mister. I came back downstairs and gazed into Mrs Cusack's plump, motherly face and said, 'Six o'clock will be grand, missis.' For a few moments I felt terribly lonely. That single word, Mister, had cut me loose from my past, from a world of schooldays and certainties, where my well-being was always somebody else's responsibility.

Now I was standing in an unfamiliar kitchen, among people I did not know, preparing to start out in life, not as ordinary, feckless and carefree Fergal, but as Mister Keane. I was also wearing a suit for the first time. As I recall, it was one of those self-important little three-pieces that men always seem to wear on their first day to work. In a week's time I would have my first pay packet – £46. Deducting £18 for bed and board and £5 for the return train home I would have £23 left for fun and foolishness. It seemed like a vast amount of money at the time and the prospect of being paid for being a reporter, something I had wanted to be since childhood, seemed to me a remarkable stroke of good fortune.

My loneliness evaporated on the bus into town as I contemplated my new-found wealth and the succession of scoops I was sure the editor would thrust into my young hands. When I actually walked in the door of the *Limerick Leader*, I was a little taken aback. The newsroom was not the grand football field-sized place of my imagination, but a small, cramped, smoky room with the desks crammed close together and eight men furiously pounding away at ancient Remington typewriters. Beyond them was another room in which a slim silver-haired man in an immaculate blue blazer and grey slacks sat puffing on a pipe and writing instructions or drawing red lines through mounds of typewritten pages.

He was the editor and his name was Brendan Halligan. He was held in awe by the rest of the staff. Born of Irish parents in England, Brendan had worked for the Thomson Group and then for the *Daily Mail*. Following the call of the blood, he had decided to come to Ireland where he married a local girl and opted for what seemed, at the time, a quieter life editing a regional newspaper. But he retained what was, to young reporters like myself, the magical aura of Fleet Street. A glimpse of the magical heights of journalism which would sustain us through long hours of tedious court reporting, or covering agricultural shows and county council meetings.

Just outside his door sat a plump figure in a blue shirt and thick glasses. He sucked on a huge cigar. 'This is Liddy,' the editor said. 'It'll be Mr Liddy to you, Keane,' said the man with the cigar.

Liddy was the sports editor and had a razor-sharp tongue and biting wit. For the first few months I lived in fear of his biting comments but we later became the best of friends. On my first day he did give me an immortal piece of advice. 'Young man, you will soon find that most of your money disappears on drink and chatting up young women,' he said. 'Happily you will find that, as a representative of this august newspaper, you are invited to numerous free lunches. When you go to these, for God's sake don't worry about the vegetables. Get stuck into the meat. Spuds you can have any time. Fillet steak is a thing to be treasured, and on your pay you'll see precious little of it.'

Later in the week I went to the Harbour Commissioners' lunch with Liddy and had the temerity to ask for *Duck à l'Orange*. 'Duck à la what?' exclaimed Liddy. The waiter faltered. Liddy looked him straight in the eye, 'He will in his arse have the duck. He'll have the steak and make it a big one.' Although there are few free lunches nowadays, I have tried to follow Liddy's advice faithfully.

Those first weeks passed in a blur. By day I would shadow one of the older reporters, by night I would struggle through shorthand and typing lessons. My first published work was a short piece about showband managers attacking the government because of a clampdown on bar extensions at dances. They correctly reasoned that, without the intoxicating benefit of vast quantities of Guinness, many of their acts would sound less than tuneful to the armies of farmers' sons and daughters who flocked to dancehalls every weekend.

The first draft came back scored through with red lines as Halligan's pen demolished words, sentences, whole paragraphs. I saw that he had cancelled out the lead sentence which said: 'The head of the Showband Managers' Federation last night lashed the government because of proposed restrictions on bar extensions.' 'What's wrong with that?' I asked timidly. 'Did you see any of these showband managers actually hitting a government minister?' he responded. I admitted that there had indeed been no physical violence at the meeting. 'Well then, never ever use that wretched cliché. Lashed. Who taught you that?' I told him I'd seen it in a national newspaper. 'Well down here there'll be no lashing. They can lash all they want in Dublin, but not here.'

By the time the third draft had been read and subbed there were only two small red lines. 'Now it's fit to print,' smiled Halligan as he wrote my first by-line on top of the story.

Working on a good local newspaper was the best of all beginnings. I covered everything and travelled every mile of the Irish midwest. Halligan had a strong social conscience and encouraged his reporters to take the side of the underdogs, even when that threatened the newspaper's lucrative and vital advertising revenue.

When a local nightclub refused to admit black students I was despatched with a photographer to capture the scene at the door when they tried to enter. When the story ran as the front-page lead the following weekend, the paper faced massive pressure from the club owners not to run a follow-up. There were anonymous calls to the paper calling me a 'nigger lover'. There were even people on the staff who advised me to ease off and let the matter lie. Halligan ignored all the pressure and encouraged me to press on. 'I'll stand by you,' he said.

And we did push on until the students received a full apology and were guaranteed admittance to the club. I wanted the apology to go on the front page as a big splash. Halligan said not. 'We have made the point. There is no need for us to gloat,' he said. As usual he was right.

Among the many things he taught me was one piece of advice I will never ever forget: 'If you are going after somebody and you believe they are in the wrong or hiding something, or that they are in some way the bad guys, then make bloody sure you get it right. There's nothing worse than people getting off the hook or being able to come back and deny everything because you have made a mistake. One inaccuracy can wreck the whole lot.'

The local reporter is answerable to his audience in a way that his counterparts on a national daily or a big broadcasting station can never be. He generally comes from the same community and will feel its praise and damnation much more acutely. On the bad provincial papers, that kind of pressure can make for very tame reporting. On the better ones, like the Limerick Leader, it forges a journalism that is responsive but also challenging. There is also a refreshing absence of pretence. The studied seriousness, the bloated self-importance which infects so many at the higher levels of journalism, tends to be much less prevalent among people who spend their time interacting with the public on a daily basis. Local reporters can influence how their city or town is run, but they are generally less likely to feel that they should be running the place instead of the elected representatives. The same cannot be said for many in the world of high journalism. Apart from anything else, there was wonderful camaraderie and fun in that small newsroom in Limerick. Anybody with pretensions was quickly cut down to size and then very painstakingly built up again. I don't know that I have ever had quite the same fun anywhere else.

One last local story: midway through my career with the *Leader* I was appointed rugby correspondent. Coming from Cork city, which was a bitter rival in rugby, I knew I would have an uphill battle convincing the hard men of the game in Limerick that I had any idea what I was talking about. For the record, Limerick rugby has a reputation for what might politely be termed 'vigour'. It is a hard game, played by hard men and, unlike in my home city of Cork, it is very much a working-class game. The home ground of one of its leading clubs rejoices in the nickname 'The Killing Fields'. Another is called 'Jurassic Park'.

I knew that my real rite of passage would come when the annual Five Nations Championship got under way and the *Limerick Leader* despatched me to Paris to cover Ireland's fortunes at the Parc des Princes. There were several local players on the national side and I would be travelling with a horde of Limerick rugby supporters. The true test of my abilities in the eyes of the fans, however, would not be measured in flowing prose or game analysis, but rather in drinking. 'As long as you buy your round and don't gawk on anyone, you'll be grand,' was the advice given by my photographer, the legendary Alfonsus 'Fonsie' Foley. Fonsie had a moustache like Pancho Villa, the cunning of a stoat, and was a veteran of many 'away' games.

The trip to France passed in a haze of alcohol and rowdy singing. I have vague memories of engaging an Algerian war veteran in a heated debate about colonialism in a miserable bar somewhere in the suburbs. Happily, Fonsie intervened in time to save my scrawny neck from being wrung by the huge paratrooper. But so great was our enthusiasm for the social side of the adventure that we neglected to collect our press tickets for the big match. It just didn't seem important in the midst of our jollification.

When the Saturday morning came, I realized through the bitter gloom of a hangover that we were ticketless. Fonsie and I raced to the headquarters of the French Rugby Union. Alas, it was too late, the little official told us, as we gasped out our names. The tickets had been allocated to somebody else. We looked at each other in horror. For the *Limerick Leader* to send us to Paris represented a major investment. Apart from the annual dinner of the Limerick Association in Chicago (which the cigar-chomping Liddy attended each year as of right), the rugby trips represented the entire foreign budget of the newspaper. Now we might be reduced to watching the game on a hotel television. I might be able to get away with that, but Fonsie would somehow have to get photographs of Limerick players.

We eventually managed to buy two grossly overpriced tickets from touts at the gate and proceeded into the ground. We were directed up a long set of stairs, and then another and another. By the time our ascent had been completed, we found ourselves sitting at the very top of the Parc des Princes. Fonsie looked at me and began to tremble. 'Mother of God, we'll see nothing from here. We're shagged,' he gasped. True enough, when the players came out of the tunnel, they seemed like tiny specks. 'They're like bloody ants down there,' muttered Fonsie. He did his best, but even with his best telephoto lens the distance was too great.

On the flight back to Limerick that night we began to panic. I could not bear the thought of facing Liddy with pathetic photographs and having to explain that drink had been our undoing. We hit on a plan. Fonsie would develop his own shots and I would take them to Liddy and play for time, while Fonsie tried to obtain pictures from another source.

I duly typed up a detailed report of the game and then galloped up to the photographic department to collect Fonsie's own shots. With trembling hands he presented the results of his effort from the top of the stand. I looked at them and gulped. They were not just bad. They were terrible. I walked back down the stairs like a man going to the gallows. I was convinced we would be fired.

Liddy sat behind his desk, the familiar cigar smoke rising above him in a malevolent cloud. 'Where is the copy and pictures?' he demanded. 'Here they are,' I said weakly. Liddy looked at each of the ten photographs, puffing intently on the cigar. 'You bloody apes,' he exploded. 'How did he take these photographs? By bloody satellite?' I told him they had been experimental shots. The ground-angle shots were on the way.

To his immense and eternal credit Liddy kept the editor and the printers at bay for an hour while Fonsie rang every photographic contact he had. It appeared hopeless. Our respective careers were in ruins. I wondered how I would explain it all to my mother who had been so proud of my appointment. Shame and penury beckoned. I think I may even have looked up the timetable for trains to Cork that evening.

And then came one of those moments of pure luck which can transform the most hopeless of situations. Fonsie was called to the phone in the photographic department. A freelance was on the line offering photographs of the match. All the national papers had sent their own people and he was having trouble off-loading his prints. 'How much do you want?' asked Fonsie. 'Pay him anything, whatever he asks for,' I whispered. Fonsie put his hand over the mouthpiece and gave me a dirty look. 'We'll have to pay for this ourselves, you clown,' he snapped. After several more minutes haggling, a deal was done. For the sum of £40, at the time an absolute fortune, we would buy his four best prints.

The images were on Liddy's desk within the hour and on the sports page of the paper three hours after that. When the first edition rolled off the presses Halligan walked into the newsroom, staring hard at the sports page. Liddy shot me a fierce look, a warning to keep quiet and let him do any explaining if there were questions. 'Gentlemen, I have only one thing to say,' said Halligan. I cringed. Had somebody told him? 'One thing to say and it's this: this is the best bloody sports page we have had all year. Lovely writing, lovely pictures and a great layout. Congratulations to all of ye,' he said, before walking back to his office, a glow of satisfaction spreading across his face.

Liddy lit his cigar and sat back, rummaging in his pockets. He produced a £20 note and threw it across to me. 'There, you gobaloon. I am sure the pictures cost you at least that. Don't open your mouth about it and don't tell Fonsie I gave you the money. He'll only think I've gone soft. Now go and have a pint and don't torment me for the rest of the day.' I thanked him profusely, took the money and walked out of the door into an afternoon that had suddenly become glorious and bright.

A CORRESPONDENT'S DIARY

Tuesday, 11 July 1995

A few days in a correspondent's life can involve a series of air flights, short stops in several countries, an important interview and some precious hours of relaxation.

It is my ninth wedding anniversary and I am sitting on a China Airlines jet bound for Burma. My wife, Anne, has cancelled the restaurant booking. 'Don't worry,' she says, 'we can do it another time.' The words have a familiar ring. With infinite patience, she has uttered them again and again in recent months. Malaysia, Papua New Guinea, Japan (three times), Korea, Thailand, Vietnam, Cambodia, the Philippines (twice) – all in the space of six months.

This latest Asian jaunt actually began last night with a news flash announcing the release of the Burmese opposition leader, Aung San Suu Kyi. The BBC's Asia office manager, Becky Evans, was on the job immediately, tracking down the necessary flights, arranging visas and money and all with a calm that helped keep everybody else in check. Now, flying south towards Thailand, I feel that old ruthless hunger – call it the predatory instinct – preparing me for the moment when we hit the ground and start working.

The cameraman is a twenty-six-year-old Australian former professional footballer, Darren Conway. He is known as DC and combines a sunny nature with splendid camerawork. I look around and notice that ITN (Independent Television News) are not on the plane. Later, we hear they went to Bangkok the night before only to find out that the Burmese embassy was closed for a holiday.

By the time we change planes for the fifty-minute flight to

Rangoon, I start feeling a little uneasy. What happens if we get turned back at the airport and ITN, by some miracle, are already in the country? If that has happened, excuses are useless. If you get beaten by the opposition, you get beaten. No amount of 'ifs' or 'buts' will make you feel better. The BBC is not exactly liked by the Burmese military dictators.

We are descending towards Rangoon. The rain is sweeping down with us on to a landscape of endless rice paddies and deep green. The policeman at the foot of the stairs waves everybody towards the arrivals terminal. Inside, I notice an ITN reporter standing just ahead of me in the queue, 'Oh God! So they did manage to get visas,' I mutter to myself. And then I hear him say: 'I'm very sorry but where can I buy a visa? I didn't have time to get one in Bangkok'.

An official is called and he leads the ITN man away. There is an intense discussion. I present my passport and visa and am allowed through. When I look back, the ITN man is gone, packed off to Bangkok on the outgoing plane.

The driver we have hired is edgy. Having been told that most people in the tourism business work for the secret police in some capacity, we are naturally reluctant to tell him what we are doing. But we need him to take us to Aung San Suu Kyi's house. There is some polite to-ing and fro-ing. 'An interesting day for Burma,' I venture. 'Oh yes, sir, an interesting day indeed,' comes the response.

Then DC has a bright idea, 'Would you like the *Post*?' he offers, handing the driver the newspaper which carries a huge front-page photograph of Aung San Suu Kyi. 'Ah the lady, the lady, the lady,' the driver responds smiling. After that the ice is broken and we are driven straight to her home.

It is raining heavily but the crowd of several hundred is undeterred. We are careful about filming too openly. There are lots of traffic policemen around, but the driver tells us not to worry. 'Everybody very relaxed, very, very relaxed,' he says. After filming and recording a few interviews we leave, but not before

I hand in my business card and a request for an interview.

The rest of the day is a nightmare. Equipment breaks down. The tape gets stuck in the camera. The flight we had planned to send our tape and voice track on does not exist. When we try instead to feed the material from the national television station, the technicians refuse to send my voice or piece to camera or any interviews. Simple censorship. By this time, I am reduced to phoning the track to London. It is the worst of all results and DC and I feel crushed.

Madeleine, at the BBC's foreign news department in London, tells us not to worry, we did our best. She means it, but she knows that whatever anybody says we will blame ourselves. We sit into the early hours reliving the day and cursing the road, the great monster that eats up our lives, pulling us along with promises of glory and then kicking us in the teeth. The road, airports, hotels, television stations. One long lonely circus. London a distant chorus of voices and demands. So it goes. After whinging for an hour or so, we go to bed, too tired to care anymore.

Wednesday, 12 July 1995

The phone is ringing, or should I say screaming into my ear. In the dark I fumble and knock a lampshade crashing to the floor. When I eventually answer, it is DC. He sounds excited, 'Her people have contacted us. We are to be there at eleven o'clock. They say she'd love to talk to us.'

The next two hours pass in a blur of wheeling and dealing. Our camera is broken. We need somebody else's camera. Eventually, we secure one from Reuters and agree to give them first bite at our interview once it has been broadcast on the BBC. It occurs to me that this will be Aung San Suu Kyi's first interview since being released from house arrest. 'Please God,' I say, 'please don't let this fall apart. Just give me this one break.'

Outside her house, a huge posse of journalists has gathered.

A Japanese photographer is strutting around arrogantly. He calls one of the gate guards aside and then points at my Reuters colleague. 'See them, those guys have nothing to offer you. Don't give them anything,' he bellows. 'Don't worry, John,' I whisper to my colleague. 'He'll get his just desserts in a few minutes.'

At exactly eleven o'clock, I walk up to the gate with DC and am admitted immediately. The first thing I notice is the overgrown garden – grass and weeds sprout up everywhere. The house is grey and crumbling. Beyond, I catch a glimpse of a lake. We are taken inside and into a room where a woman, who is sitting at the table, suddenly turns around and says 'So you are here'.

Aung San Suu Kyi looks at least twenty years younger than her stated age of fifty. She is petite and very polite, but her eyes pulse energy and she speaks in fast vital sentences. She tells me that she used to listen to my reports from South Africa all the time when she was under house arrest. My voice had brought her the story of that country's transformation from a racist autocracy. I am taken aback by this and humbled.

How do you listen to one of the living heroes of our age praising your work without blushing? The simple answer is that you don't. She recalls one of my reports on From Our Own Correspondent, when I described a visit to the scene of a massacre in Rwanda. 'That place, it was called Nyarabuye, was it not?' she asks. 'It was. That is correct. What excellent recall,' I reply.

We speak for nearly two hours. As an interviewee, Aung San Suu Kyi is like a gale of fresh air. No evasion, no hiding behind semantics or statistics. For the first time since arriving in Asia, I feel something of the old passion and clarity that I felt in South Africa at the best of times.

We speak about freedom as an idea. She tells me that the regime could not take away the freedom in her heart and mind and soul. Later, as I am preparing to leave, she tells me to write to her. 'Write and tell us when we are going wrong,' she says.

As a foreign correspondent, I am always conscious of the

need to maintain what I call a 'necessary distance' between the subject and the claims of my own emotions. But in doing this, one does not become an unfeeling robot. So now, away from the world of hard news, here in these highly personalized columns, I can tell you that Aung San Suu Kyi came across as one of the warmest human beings I have ever met. True, she is a political leader and in time she might have to take unpopular decisions, might take the wrong ones. But her humanity, her breadth of vision and her courage were truly inspiring.

That night we fly out to Bangkok and satellite all thirty-five minutes of the interview. It is a world exclusive. By the time we finish feeding, it is the early hours. We are too tired to celebrate and we munch our way through plates of room-service sandwiches. I ring my wife and wish her happy anniversary.

Tuesday, 25 July 1995

Ardmore, County Waterford, Republic of Ireland: I have spooled forward through the days and am relaxing on the south-east coast of Ireland. In the meantime, there has been another trip to Burma. Aung San Suu Kyi looks tired this time. She is worn down by the media pressures.

The Director-General of the BBC, John Birt, has visited Hong Kong for a few days. China is flexing its muscles with Taiwan and the Sri Lanka war escalates. But now that I am here in the village where my great-grandfather was a policeman, I am starting to unwind, to put some distance between me and the job.

Ardmore is one of the oldest Christian settlements in Ireland with a round tower and an ancient monastery. It has beautiful wide beaches, secret coves and leafy lanes thick with brambles and honeysuckle. I know it as a place that was a happy refuge in childhood, where I learned to swim and fish, went to my first dances and fell in love for the first time. Each summer I would travel down to Ardmore by train and bus from Dublin to be met by my grandmother, a great warm woman who taught me what wisdom I have.

In a life that is notable for its dislocation, its endless rushing around, Ardmore is a symbol of continuity. It roots me to a place that has been part of my family's history for generations. The people are not interested in what I do or what awards I have won. They take me for who I am. Because I spend most of the year in an environment where I am seen first and foremost as a BBC correspondent, it is a pleasure to be known as just me.

The cottage is called Wayside and is our sole property. It has one bedroom, a tiny dining-room, a sitting-room, kitchen and bathroom. It was built in the 1930s and is a place of sunshine and birdsong. Its former owner told us that Fred Astaire was once a guest. The garden is large and I will lounge here every morning reading and sipping coffee.

In the afternoon, my Uncle Paul arrives with a small fishing boat I have purchased. Paul is the family boat expert and found the vessel for me. But Ardmore Bay is choppy this evening; the weather on the western side of the headland is better. After much debate, we decide to launch the boat at Whiting Bay, some two miles to the west. It is calm there.

We are joined by cousins, friends, neighbours. We heave and shove. The water is icy cold. The last time I stepped in the sea water was the Philippines. There it was crystal clear and warm. What matter? This is home and the laughter of friends and family is singing in my ears.

Before too long the engine has been started and I am steering the boat across Whiting Bay. There is a long night ahead. Back at Wayside, a feast is being prepared. We will talk into the early hours. Perhaps we will sing. Uncle Paul has an Irish tenor voice that would melt the hardest heart. Our neighbour, Jimmy Maloney, will tell stories about the old Ardmore. And then we will sleep and no phones will ring, and, for a few sweet weeks, my life will be my own.

LETTER TO MY FATHER

Cork, December 1995

Eamon Patrick Keane died on 5 January 1990.

Behind the bedroom door you are sleeping. I can hear your snores rattling down the stairs to our ruined sitting-room. Here among the broken chairs, the overturned Christmas tree, we are preparing to leave you. We are breaking away from you, Da.

Last night you crashed through the silence, dead drunk and spinning in your own wild orbit into another year of dreams. This would be the year of the big break – of Hollywood, you said. Oh, my actor father, time was, time was we swallowed those lines, but no longer.

Before leaving I look into the bedroom to where your hand droops out from under the covers, below it the small empty Powers' bottle, and I say goodbye. And at seven o'clock on New Year's Day we push the old Ford Anglia down the driveway, my mother, brother and I. We push because the engine might wake you, and none of us can face a farewell scene. I don't know what the neighbours think, if anything, when they see a woman and two small boys stealing away in the grey morning, but I don't care, we're heading south with everything we own.

The day I turned twelve, which was four days later, you called to say happy birthday. You were, as I remember, halfway sober, but you didn't say much else, except to ask for my mother who would not come to the phone.

In the background I could hear glasses clinking, voices raised, and you said: 'Tell her I love her,' and then the change ran out, and I began to understand what made love the saddest word in any language.

Christmas that year you had access to the children. We met in Cork station. I remember your new suit, your embarrassed embrace, the money you pressed into our hands, and the smell of whiskey. We found a taxi and the driver stared at us, throwing his eyes to heaven and shaking his head.

What I see now are many such faces: the waitress at the Old Bridge Café where drinks were spilled; the couple who asked for an autograph and watched your shaking hand struggle to write, before they beat a mortified retreat. And on through pubs and bookmakers' shops to one last café where Elvis was crooning 'Love Me Tender, Love Me Sweet' on an ancient radio. By now, nobody was able to speak.

There was a taxi ride home, we children in the back, you in the front, and what lives with me still, always, is the moment of leave-taking, Christmas 1972. Because, as the car drove you away from our lives, I saw through the steamed-up windows that your eyes had become waterfalls.

I was too young to understand what you knew – that we were lost to you, broken away. Down the years we struggled to find one another, but I was growing up and away, and you were drifting closer to darkness. And at the end I gave up writing, gave up calling. I gave up. Until one night my cousin called to say you were gone. It was a few days into the New Year, and your heart simply gave up in a small room in the town in north Kerry where you were born. I remember that you sent me the collected stories of Raymond Carver for Christmas. I had sent you nothing, not even a card. Now I would send you a thousand, but I have no address.

LETTER TO DANIEL

Hong Kong, February 1996

Daniel Patrick Keane was born on 4 February, 1996.

My dear son, it is six o'clock in the morning on the island of Hong Kong. You are asleep cradled in my left arm and I am learning the art of one-handed typing. Your mother, more tired yet more happy than I've ever known her, is sound asleep in the room next door and there is soft quiet in our apartment.

Since you've arrived, days have melted into night and back again and we are learning a new grammar, a long sentence whose punctuation marks are feeding and winding and nappy changing and these occasional moments of quiet.

When you're older we'll tell you that you were born in Britain's last Asian colony in the lunar year of the pig and that when we brought you home, the staff of our apartment block gathered to wish you well. "It's a boy, so lucky, so lucky. We Chinese love boys," they told us. One man said you were the first baby to be born in the block in the year of the pig. This, he told us, was good Feng Shui, in other words a positive sign for the building and everyone who lived there.

Naturally your mother and I were only too happy to believe that. We had wanted you and waited for you, imagined you and dreamed about you and now that you are here no dream can do justice to you. Outside the window, below us on the harbour, the ferries are ploughing back and forth to Kowloon. Millions are already up and moving about and the sun is slanting through the tower blocks and out on to the flat silver waters of the South China Sea. I can see the contrail of a jet over Lamma Island and, somewhere out there, the last stars flickering towards the other side of the world.

We have called you Daniel Patrick but I've been told by my Chinese friends that you should have a Chinese name as well and this glorious dawn sky makes me think we'll call you Son of the Eastern Star. So that later, when you and I are far from Asia, perhaps standing on a beach some evening, I can point at the sky and tell you of the Orient and the times and the people we knew there in the last years of the twentieth century.

Your coming has turned me upside down and inside out. So much that seemed essential to me has, in the past few days, taken on a different colour. Like many foreign correspondents I know, I have lived a life that, on occasion, has veered close to the edge: war zones, natural disasters, darkness in all its shapes and forms.

In a world of insecurity and ambition and ego, it's easy to be drawn in, to take chances with our lives, to believe that what we do and what people say about us is reason enough to gamble with death. Now, looking at your sleeping face, inches away from me, listening to your occasional sigh and gurgle, I wonder how I could have ever thought glory and prizes and praise were sweeter than life.

And it's also true that I am pained, perhaps haunted is a better word, by the memory, suddenly so vivid now, of each suffering child I have come across on my journeys. To tell you the truth, it's nearly too much to bear at this moment to even think of children being hurt and abused and killed. And yet looking at you, the images come flooding back. Ten-year-old Andi Mikail dying from napalm burns on a hillside in Eritrea, how his voice cried out, growing ever more faint when the wind blew dust on to his wounds. The two brothers, Domingo and Juste, in Menongue, southern Angola. Juste, two years old and blind, dying from malnutrition, being carried on seven-year-old Domingo's back. And Domingo's words to me, 'He was nice before, but now he has the hunger'.

Last October, in Afghanistan, when you were growing inside your mother, I met Sharja, aged twelve. Motherless, fatherless, guiding me through the grey ruins of her home, everything was gone, she told me. And I knew that, for all her tender years, she had learned more about loss than I would likely understand in a lifetime.

There is one last memory. Of Rwanda, and the churchyard of the parish of Nyarabuye where, in a ransacked classroom, I found a mother and her three young children huddled together where they'd been beaten to death. The children had died holding on to their mother, that instinct we all learn from birth and in one way or another cling to until we die.

Daniel, these memories explain some of the fierce protectiveness I feel for you, the tenderness and the occasional moments of blind terror when I imagine anything happening to you. But there is something more, a story from long ago that I will tell you face to face, father to son, when you are older. It's a very personal story but it's part of the picture. It has to do with the long lines of blood and family, about our lives and how we can get lost in them and, if we're lucky, find our way out again into the sunlight.

It begins thirty-five years ago in a big city on a January morning with snow on the ground and a woman walking to hospital to have her first baby. She is in her early twenties and the city is still strange to her, bigger and noisier than the easy streets and gentle hills of her distant home. She's walking because there is no money and everything of value has been pawned to pay for the alcohol to which her husband has become addicted.

On the way, a taxi driver notices her sitting, exhausted and cold, in the doorway of a shop and he takes her to hospital for free. Later that day, she gives birth to a baby boy and, just as you are to me, he is the best thing she has ever seen. Her husband comes that night and weeps with joy when he sees his son. He is truly happy. Hungover, broke, but in his own way happy, for they were both young and in love with each other and their son.

But, Daniel, time had some bad surprises in store for them. The cancer of alcoholism ate away at the man and he lost his family. This was not something he meant to do or wanted to do, it just was. When you are older, my son, you will learn about how complicated life becomes, how we can lose our way and how people get hurt inside and out. By the time his son had grown up, the man lived away from his family, on his own in a one-roomed flat, living and dying for the bottle.

He died on the fifth of January, one day before the anniversary of his son's birth, all those years before in that snowbound city. But his son was too far away to hear his last words, his final breath, and all the things they might have wished to say to one another were left unspoken.

Yet now, Daniel, I must tell you that when you let out your first powerful cry in the delivery room of the Adventist Hospital and I became a father, I thought of your grandfather and, foolish though it may seem, hoped that in some way he could hear, across the infinity between the living and the dead, your proud statement of arrival. For if he could hear, he would recognize the distinct voice of family, the sound of hope and new beginnings that you and all your innocence and freshness have brought to the world.

A DOG'S LIFE

Hong Kong, June 1996

The foreign correspondent's life may seem, to some at any rate, a glamorous one, but that's a view certainly not shared by any pets he or she might have.

Something about our domestic helper's face told me she had suffered a bad shock. Her mouth opened to speak, but then closed again, the words choked off somewhere behind her tonsils. 'What's wrong?' I asked. She shook her head and then sat down. It took me a full ten minutes to extract the terrible truth and when it came it was indeed terrible. But first, before I can tell you what happened, a little background.

Aprila, who comes from the Philippines, has grown terribly fond of our two dogs, Sam and Susie. The former, a longhaired retriever, the latter, a plump (well, actually, fat) black labrador. Much of Susie's plumpness can be attributed to the rather generous, to put it mildly, helpings of dog food which Aprila doles out several times a day. Susie is an eating machine and, although smaller than Sam, frequently elbows, or should I say paws, him out of the way when it comes to mealtimes. He stands there looking forlorn until I manage to get Susie's guzzling face out of his dish.

But as countless Catholic priests told me in my youth, there's a price to be paid for every sin, and for Susie's sin of gluttony there was to be a reckoning. Well, actually, in her case, there turned out to be two reckonings. The first came when Aprila was taking the dogs for a morning walk and noticed a Filipino gardener on the corner, staring hard in her direction. He seemed to be leering. For a moment, she wondered if she was the object of his hungry gaze and then she noticed that he was, in fact, looking at Susie. As Aprila and the hounds turned the corner she heard him call out 'How much for the fat one?' 'She's not for sale,' she replied. 'Are you sure? Boy, she'd make such good eating. So fat, so much meat,' he exclaimed.

When I heard this later I thanked God that, to the best of my knowledge, my dogs had no understanding of Tagalog, the principal language of the Philippines, the language in which this vile transaction was proposed. Aprila grasped their leashes tighter and broke into a trot, quickly putting a healthy distance between Susie and her gourmet admirer. I should not have been surprised. Dogs are a dinner-table special in many parts of Asia but the thought of dear Susie with her soulful brown eyes and endlessly wagging tail, the thought of her lying on a silver platter with an apple in her mouth, all because we had fattened her into a prize delicacy, the thought was, frankly, too much to bear.

There was, of course, only one solution to all of this. Unhappily, the solution brought Susie paw-to-paw with her next reckoning. After emergency consultations with Aprila and my wife, we decided that a diet and a programme of rigorous exercises were needed. Susie would have to lose her flabby flanks and, with any luck, I might lose a few of the pounds which have prompted several of my more unkind friends to refer to me as Bunter.

And so, on a steaming hot Sunday afternoon, I set forth with some dog-loving friends for a long walk along one of the pathways in the hills above Hong Kong. Below us the city spread out towards China in a vast sea of superlatives which I won't bore you with. Joggers pounded past us. You know the kind: mid-twenties, all Nike and Walkmans and rippling muscles, the new puritans of the sensible nineties, freed from the red braces, the twinsets and the multiple tyrannies of the dealing room floor for a few hours on a hot Sunday. I noticed that most of them scowled at the dogs as they went past.

We had just turned off the main track on to a quieter path and allowed the dogs off the leash when Susie pounced on a piece of barbecued meat lying in the grass. It was devoured in milli-seconds. All was well until we reached the end of the walk and I said goodbye to my friends. Then, without warning, Susie was transformed from a happy panting dog into a writhing, howling, foaming beast. She collapsed on her side and was sick repeatedly, twisting and turning in terrible pain.

I frantically waved down taxis but none would stop. A bus came, but refused to allow me to get on with the animals. Overcome with fear I began to walk but Susie could hardly even stagger. Night was coming on and my home was a good five sweltering miles away across the mountain. Besides, I was supposed to be catching a plane to Australia to film a story. I picked up my mobile phone, the battery was dead. I looked around frantically for a public telephone, none to be seen. There was nothing for it but to pick the dog up in my arms and begin the long trek home.

I got there hours later feeling more dead than alive, covered in dog vomit, and rang the vet, breathlessly describing the symptoms. 'She's obviously been poisoned,' he said, 'but if she's managed to survive this long she'll pull through.' His advice was to starve her for twenty-four hours, give her lots of water and then come and see him tomorrow when she had slept. There had been lots of similar poisonings, he told me. The rumour was that a crazed jogger, someone who had been chased by dogs one time too many, had started placing poisoned meat along the track. Several animals had been killed, in fact. Susie was very lucky, he said.

And so I cancelled the flight to Australia and played nurse to my whimpering hound for the night. She slept in her basket, I nearby on the couch. In the middle of the night I heard a few yelps and looked across. Susie was asleep, lost in some dog dream. Was she dreaming of her home in Africa? Of the highveld in the winter and the guinea fowl rising in clouds as she chased after them? Maybe. Maybe she was actually cursing me in her dreams for having brought her to these alien Asian shores. I felt guilty for about two seconds and then went back to sleep.

At about six in the morning I was woken by a curious sensation; something warm and sandpapery was licking my face, and I was aware of the malodorous whiff of dog breath drifting over me. I opened my eyes. Susie was sitting there, eyes bright, tail wagging, and I could have sworn she was saying 'Breakfast please'. Poor Susie, much too old to learn new tricks.

Part Two

AFRICA

AN OLD STORY OF AFRICA

Kinshasa, October 1991

Violence and looting on the streets of the Zairean capital brought further criticism of the rule of President Mobutu, but no improvement to the lives of his people.

The door opened and the muzzle of a rifle poked its way enquiringly into the stuffy interior of the aircraft. Within seconds another gun followed, and after that a face hidden behind ludicrously large and menacing sunglasses. The face barked at us in French, 'Who are you? What are you doing here?' It was momentarily mollified by the offer of a cigarette, but soon returned to the interrogation.

As the questions continued I noticed a long line of refugees walking across the runway, guarded by several huge Belgian and French paratroopers; they were clutching suitcases and plastic bags and small children, some looking anxiously over their shoulders at the Zairean troops skulking around our plane. It was a scene from an old newsreel circa 1960: terrified whites fleeing the oncoming darkness and leaving behind everything that could not be carried.

After about two hours we begged our guards to let us go to the toilet. They did so and we, all of us, regretted asking: the airport had been completely ransacked in the mutiny and the toilets were now ankle-deep in human waste; in the stifling heat the odour was overpowering. On the way back I noticed that all of the Zairean forces were wearing blue headsets, but there were no Walkmans attached. The headsets had apparently been looted from aircraft stores, and although useless without tape recorders, they were, apparently, a status symbol of sorts.

Eventually we were allowed out of the aircraft, largely

thanks to the resourcefulness of a Parisian colleague from Reuters who had given the Zaireans an impressive list of relatives serving with the French Military. We were shown to a room where another group of surly guards took over until a certain Colonel Ndoma of the Presidential Guard arrived to say, to our great amazement, that we were welcome.

An hour later we were sitting with the Information Minister, Monsieur Danza, under a huge portrait of President Mobutu. Monsieur Danza was a plump man with a clammy handshake and an oily sincerity; he held in his hand a cellular telephone which, in President Mobutu's new Zaire, seemed to represent the very essence of civilization and modern values.

There were quite a few such people in Kinshasa – men who sported expensive suits and gold chains, the inner circle that has grown prosperous under one of the most corrupt dictatorships the world has ever seen. Kinshasa was full too of nervous soldiers who, for $20, would willingly leave their posts to provide you with an escort through the dangerous night-time streets, past the skeletons of shops ravaged in the rioting, through roadblocks manned by other nervous soldiers. It was packed as well with hungry people, angry people who would surround you in the slums and castigate the European forces for preserving Mobutu's regime; with children who would stand on the roadside rubbing their stomachs and begging for food. 'Mobutu is Lucifer!' the crowd at one crossroads shouted.

Little wonder these people scavenged in the deserted shops. Theirs was a looting born of physical hunger and, in many cases, a looting that simply followed the long example of their overlords, who had plundered for years, except they had done it, more often than not, with pens and handshakes, dispatching vast sums into Swiss bank accounts and into foreign property holdings.

Out at the Presidential Palace, or should I say one of

the presidential palaces, the dictator dined with the opposition on smoked salmon and champagne. Down in the slums people struggled desperately to keep from starvation. It was an old story of Africa, but none the less sorry for that. Mobutu himself was charismatic in a deeply unsettling way, his head slowly turning to face me when I asked how he was feeling. 'Obviously not a hundred per cent. What did you expect?' he growled in reply. Everywhere he went in the conference centre a white aide followed, fluttering around him like a moth transfixed by light.

The whole scene, the whole week, reminded me of V.S. Naipaul's magnificent evocation of the dictator and his cronies in his novel, *A Bend in the River*: 'They didn't see, these young men, that there was anything there to build in their country. As far as they were concerned it was all there already; they only had to take, they believed that by being who they were they had earned the right to take; and the higher the office, the greater the crookedness – if that word had any meaning.'

As I conclude, the opposition are locked in conflict with Mobutu. The French and Belgians still patrol the streets and the price of basic foodstuffs continues to rocket. Of the future one can only predict that, for the ordinary people of Zaire, it will be as hard and as difficult as it has always been – a continuing struggle against impossible odds.

DRY WHITE SEASON

Johannesburg, February 1992

South Africa suffered the effects of what was described as its worst
drought this century. Crops failed and thousands of cattle were
slaughtered because there was no feed for them. All of this
coincided with a by-election campaign during which President
de Klerk hoped to convince his white Afrikaner
constituency that his dismantling of apartheid was the only
way forward for the country.

It is just after sunrise here in the privileged avenues of north
Johannesburg – impossibly dull suburbs where, just about
now, the water sprinklers are starting to shower the parched
lawns with precious drops of moisture. It is a curiously beautiful hour of the morning. The birds are singing, the traffic has
yet to rumble into action and the air is still cool.

As I write, the voices of the other real Africa are beginning
to stir in houses along the road. They are the voices of maids,
gardeners, and security guards. It is one of the few hours of
these drought days when movement is not calculated to bring
the perspiration rushing to one's brow.

Not very far away, across the so-called Golden Highway that
encircles the city, out where the veld begins, the farmers and
their labourers will be up and about, anxious to work
the land before the sun begins to dry the air and burn the skin.
As they move through the fields of maize there will be a
crunching sound underfoot and a brittle scratching noise as the
withering leaves brush against the clothes of the workers. Little
clouds of dust will rise and hang on the air. And ever more
quickly the temperature will start to rise, out of the sweet cool-
ness and into the sticky regions of mid-morning. It has been the

same every day for weeks upon end – the 'Dry White Season' evoked by the South African novelist André Brink.

Drive in any direction from Johannesburg and you will encounter the effects of this torrid unrelenting dryness. It has seized the land by the throat and is slowly, from the fields of the Orange Free State, up into the ranchland of southern Zimbabwe, draining its strength away. In a cattle market in the western Transvaal, I saw truck after truck draw up, depositing animals that could no longer be fed. The farmers told me it was the worst drought that any of them could remember, a curse that would drive them to the unfamiliar and frightening cities to compete for jobs with black people who had for so long been their servants.

The manager of the hotel in the small industrial town of Potchefstroom some forty miles south-west of Johannesburg told me of how many farmers had given up the ghost. They sat in his bar all day as their fields yielded to the sustained assault of the sun, and the debts piled up. 'Whether they owe a hundred rand or a hundred thousand they don't seem to care,' he told me. By the week's end there was an air of barely subdued panic.

Apart from the very real and sad human consequences, this drought has proved an important factor in the political sphere. The farmers, never the most liberal of South Africa's citizens, are blaming their woes on the government at a time when President de Klerk is fighting what is probably the most crucial by-election in South African history. Little wonder that, when he faced the voters of Potchefstroom during the week, the President had to remind them that the government was not responsible for the drought or any other natural disaster. I'm not sure they believed him: the Afrikaner people have an instinctual faith in what they perceive to be warnings from the Almighty: the unholy drought falls into this category.

The Conservative Party has been canvassing the farmers relentlessly, offering them the promise of green pastures in a white homeland. It must be a tempting offer when you are gazing out on withering fields. The Nationalists, by contrast, have seemed almost apologetic in their campaigning, urging people to stick with them simply because there is no alternative. In terms of logic there can be little doubting the veracity of the Nationalist argument. In no part of South Africa do whites form an absolute majority. Therefore any talk of a white fatherland is unrealistic in the extreme. But then these are extreme times and the Conservative offer of a return to the simple certainties of apartheid finds ready acceptance in the drought-stricken hinterland.

In the Party's campaign office in Potchefstroom there was an air of self-satisfied assuredness. A stern *vrou*, ferrying a tray of tea and a slab of cake to the candidate, paused to tell me, 'We have it sown up, sonny. F.W. is going to get his answer here.'

Certainly President de Klerk did not help his own cause by taking off on a tour of Europe while his candidate in Potchefstroom struggled in the face of the most organized Conservative campaign ever. It fed the perception of many ordinary Afrikaners that President de Klerk was more interested in gathering foreign accolades than explaining to them why their world was being turned upside down.

Yet, for all that, I believe that this election is too close to call. De Klerk's own speech in Potchefstroom, reminding whites that they were a minority, helped to inject a degree of realism into a campaign dominated by wild fears and even wilder promises. The Conservatives have also come unstuck whenever they have been asked to define the borders of the white homeland: the impossible dream that successive generations of Afrikaners have searched for in the wilderness.

The morning paper arrived a short time ago. Like everybody else these days I turned first to the weather section. It promised yet more heat, dust and drought, more withered crops and only the vaguest rumours of rain.

A NEW DAWN

Cape Town, March 1992

White voters gave an overwhelming endorsement to President de Klerk's reforms, paving the way for an end to white minority rule. The President won more than seventy per cent of the vote in the whites-only referendum, well ahead of expectations. It was an extraordinary moment in South African history.

The day is clear and sunny and the waters of Table Bay are sparkling in the distance. From the jagged shapes of the Hottentots-Holland mountains, carving around the coast to Blouburg Strand, there is an extraordinary calm. It was on a day such as this that Jan Van Reibeeck's ships loomed on the horizon, edging in from the Atlantic to cast their long shadow across the southern half of Africa. The poet John Masefield, writing of Columbus, called the ships of the explorers 'doom burdened caravels', recognizing that what they carried with them was the beginning of a new order, the order of the white man.

On the southern tip of Africa, as in the Americas, history was to roll across the plains, mountains and rivers, subjugating or annihilating anything which stood in the way. For the native peoples of South Africa, it amounted to a catastrophe as the white man drove back the horizon. The tribes of the Cape were either annihilated or forced into slavery.

Trekking further into the wilderness, the whites defeated black tribe after tribe. Defeat and humiliation became by-words. For whites, it was a pathway to unimagined privilege, but also fear and isolation. As the world moved forward they languished in the seventeenth century, despised and rejected. As they inflicted a code of racial supremacy on the black man, so the world inflicted its moral apartheid on them. They were of Africa, yet had cut themselves off from it. They yearned for the fellowship of nations, yet were shut out.

That was until yesterday. In one great leap, the whites came back to Africa and the world. It was not only F.W. de Klerk's triumph, it was a victory for ordinary people, because the choice to reject racism and embrace peaceful co-existence was a deeply personal one. Implicit in the 'yes' vote was a recognition of Anthony Trollope's wise dictum that South Africa was a country of black people and always would be. No re-drawing of borders would ever change that fact.

For any of us to reject the certainties with which we have grown up is difficult. It involves a measure of risk that most people would shy away from. That is what makes yesterday's vote so remarkable, because the people who voted 'yes' grew up with apartheid. Leader after leader told them it was the only way in which to ensure the survival of the white race. Racial separation marked every aspect of their lives. It was not something that could be taken or left.

In the light of this we should not be too surprised that nearly thirty per cent of whites felt unable to leave the past behind. They are not all of them raving racists, not all 'bitter-enders' and certainly not all potential soldiers in Mr Terre' Blanche's promised war of liberation. For the most part, I suspect, they are frightened people who have yet to begin the journey to realism.

Now that the cause for which they campaigned has been well and truly lost it is difficult to believe that the Right can sustain a concerted fight against the inevitable. Some will doubtless try to stain the future with blood. Most though will, in some way or other, come to terms with the demands of survival, realizing that a loss of political control does not necessarily mean losing a way of life. The more pragmatic in the ranks of the Right will almost certainly come to the negotiating table, whatever taunts of traitor and sell-out may come from the extremists.

A decade ago when I first visited this country there was a defensiveness and an arrogance about many whites that filled me with despair. After a while, I learnt to avoid arguments on the subject of apartheid; they invariably led nowhere. South Africa was a depressing place to be. The heavy hand of the state was demolishing organized opposition, the border war was rumbling on and Liberals were wringing their hands in despair.

Back then, it would have been impossible to imagine a white president standing on the steps of parliament and congratulating his people for voting an end to minority rule. And yet, now that it has happened, there is less a sense of surprise or amazement than there is of relief. It is as if the South African nation breathed out a long sigh yesterday and blew away the foul dust of history.

THE LORD OF CISKEI

Bisho, September 1992

More than thirty supporters of the African National Congress
were shot dead after they confronted troops in the Ciskei
homeland. But the incident did lead to a new summit meeting
between the ANC and the South African government which paved
the way for full constitutional talks.

The photograph shows a small schoolboyish face gazing out
rather uncertainly from under an outsized officer's hat. The
headgear and the accompanying uniform are heavily decorat-
ed with braiding and badges. When you see his face on television, as the citizens of Ciskei most often do, you notice
something extraordinarily furtive about his eyes. They seem to
dart around, avoiding prolonged contact with other eyes,
and give the impression of a man uniquely ill at ease with his
rank and situation. But Brigadier Oupa Gqozo is lord of all he
surveys in Ciskei, from the new-town ugliness of the capital
Bisho to the townships and villages that dot this dubious
tribute to Verwoerd and his strategy of grand apartheid.

Ciskei was intended to be one of two homelands for the
Xhosa people, South Africa's second most populous tribe. Like
its neighbour Transkei, which is ruled by an ANC-supporting
dictator, Ciskei is not recognized internationally. It is seen by
the international community for the fiction that it is. Sure
enough, Ciskei has its own flag, its own embassy in Pretoria, its
own parliament building, and, most vital of all for a state which
lacks the support of its citizenry, a heavily armed defence force.

I first encountered these soldiers on a side road after I had
crossed the invisible border from South Africa. About twenty
men in camouflage uniforms, cradling automatic rifles, were

lounging by the side of the road. As I drove past, they waved and cheered, perhaps assuming I was one of the South African military intelligence officers who helped Brigadier Gqozo keep his despotic circus on the road. Nearer to Bisho the numbers of soldiers standing by the roadside, manning roadblocks, grew. All of the state buildings were heavily defended. Armoured troop carriers, with heavy machine guns mounted on their prows, rumbled along the streets.

Eventually I reached the stadium, scene of the shootings of the previous day. The soldiers here were tense and unfriendly. I have met many like them in the other military states of Africa; overarmed, underpaid and sullen. As I drove toward the stadium, one or two of the troops lying in the bush started gesticulating and warning me away. Something about their behaviour convinced me that arguments about democracy and freedom of the press might be fruitless. These were men who had, only a short time before, turned their guns on an unarmed crowd.

Looking at them, at their menace, I wondered what kind of lunacy must have gripped those ANC marchers who broke away from the main crowd and ran towards the troops. Had they forgotten the reputation for brutality which the Ciskei security forces enjoy? Had the memory of the 1990 shootings of ten supporters at a similar rally faded away? I had only to conclude that, as much as the Ciskei forces and their leaders were brutish and callous, the ANC demonstrators and their leader Mr Ronnie Kasrils, who led the charge, were at best woefully naive, at worst dangerously provocative.

What happened at Bisho was ultimately the fault of the system of apartheid which created dictators like Gqozo and his ANC-supporting neighbour in Transkei, General Bantu Holomisa. The system spawned a complete disregard for democracy, and encouraged avarice, patronage and a contempt for human rights. To shoot to kill is as natural as daylight for a military or a police force which has never had to answer for itself.

To those of us present in Bisho in the aftermath of the killings there was no tangible sense of guilt, even remorse, on the part of the Brigadier and his troops. Indeed, in one unbelievable statement, Brigadier Gqozo told the BBC his troops had acted with the utmost restraint. Later his press office released a copy of the Brigadier's curriculum vitae. It contained several nuggets. The best though was the glowing tribute to the Brigadier's record on human rights, a concept he was strongly committed to, the statement said.

But now that the ANC and the government appear to be set to talk again, one is forced to accept that the Bisho massacre appears to have acted as a catalyst. As Aziz Pahad of the ANC remarked, it seems to have jolted everybody to their senses. That, one is bound to say, is of little comfort to the relatives and friends of the more than thirty people who died. Like most victims of South Africa's violence, these were ordinary people, the poor and the dispossessed. Their grieving relatives are unlikely to forgive the politicians if they walk away from the summit meeting without having rescued South Africa from its slide into the abyss.

THE DIRTY TRICKS MAN

Johannesburg, November 1992

President F.W. de Klerk ordered an investigation into
disclosures by Judge Richard Goldstone that the army had
hired a known killer to conduct a dirty tricks campaign
against the ANC.

We were huddled together outside the main door of the
Johannesburg Sun Hotel, keeping a wary eye out for the
muggers who infest its precincts. Just beyond us, innocent
tourists rambled along, blissfully oblivious of the criminal
piranhas who lurk on almost every city-centre street corner.

It was a hot afternoon on an ordinary scandal-filled day in
this new South Africa; we – about twenty or so journalists –
were waiting for one Ferdinand Barnard, a killer, a thief and
generally nasty individual. He had been catapulted to fame in
the previous twenty-four hours with the disclosure that the
South African military intelligence had hired him to carry out
a dirty tricks campaign aimed at the ANC.

As we loitered, a car drew up and a tall fair-haired man
jumped out. He introduced himself as one Calla Botha, a former member of the notorious CCB, a state hit-squad with a
history of assassinations and dirty tricks. Calla had come to be
with his friend Ferdi when he met the press. Something about
this brawny Afrikaner frightened and fascinated me at the
same time. I suspected there was much he could tell us, but of
course he was retaining the right to remain silent. A persuasive
colleague did manage to coax him into saying a few words
about the still absent Ferdi. He was, explained Calla, a sensitive
and loyal person. That was the real Ferdi Barnard; not, he
might have added, the murderer and dirty tricks expert.

Not long afterwards, sensitive and loyal Ferdi strode into view, fresh from a nearby courthouse where he is being questioned about the murder of an anti-apartheid activist in 1989. He was, if you will forgive the pun, dressed to kill: designer suit, floral tie and head held high. We clambered after him: up escalators, into lifts, emerging into the sunlight of the hotel's rooftop bar.

What followed was one of those classic moments when a person of, to put it mildly, dubious background attempts to convince his questioners that he really is a man of good character whose only crime was loyalty. He told us he was being made a scapegoat, that people in the intelligence community were out to get him, he even had to move his family because of fears of attack. And, predictably, he denied that his plan had ever been accepted by the military.

Wasn't this simply an attempt to save his own skin? I asked him. 'No way,' said Ferdi, 'not at all.' I cannot say I found the performance convincing, but then a convicted killer and shady character of Ferdi Barnard's ilk would have had difficulty convincing us that it was daytime, were we not able to see it for our own eyes.

What I could accept, to some degree, was that Ferdi was the scapegoat. He was at least here in the open answering questions, his name and photograph were in every paper in the land, his past dreadful deeds widely publicized. There was very little about himself he could hide, even if he wanted to. That was not the case with the faceless generals – the men who appointed and controlled Barnard in spite of his past record. No, these men, as they have done for years, sat secure in their bases in Pretoria beyond the reach of the media, and, it seems, the law.

As I write, President de Klerk has appointed another general to investigate them, a move that can hardly be said to inspire confidence in an impartial inquiry. For the best part of two decades the generals have acted without regard to any principle save the maintenance of white power and the suppression of black dissent. They were encouraged, aided and abetted by politicians who were either as ruthless as they were, or perhaps in some cases scared of them. They are the architects of the total onslaught theory, which put forward the notion of a black communist avalanche preparing to crush Christian white South Africa. An onslaught which had to be stopped by any means, fair or foul.

On the evidence available these generals had a particular weakness for foul means. The history of recent years is littered with examples of dirty tricks and assassination squads killing and corrupting with impunity. That their dirty deeds are now coming into the open is perhaps a natural consequence of the decline of white power, the crumbling of the monolith, but also a consequence of the determined efforts of a few good men. I refer here to people like Judge Richard Goldstone and his investigators, particularly those investigators seconded from the South African police. It was they who uncovered the latest scandal and who had the courage to damn the political consequences and proceed with their inquiries.

At a time of general disillusionment, of serious questions about the integrity of the whole process of negotiation, there is at least some comfort to be drawn from the presence of Judge Goldstone and his brave colleagues.

MAP-MAKERS OF APARTHEID

Johannesburg, January 1993

In South Africa, the borders began at your boundary wall.
Apartheid and the creation of independent tribal republics had
resulted in fear and alienation. And, although the policies of
separation were fast becoming discredited, the map-makers of
apartheid had carved division into every facet of life.

It is late evening and the light is leaving Johannesburg north,
fading out into the improbable vastness of Africa. As the darkness intensifies the security lights of houses along the road
flicker into life. Behind the high walls, vicious dogs are on the
prowl; revolvers are taken out of bedroom safes and tucked
under pillows while each steel gate becomes a border.

Sometimes I stand in the garden after dark listening to the
voices of Africa laughing, shouting, crying on the other side of
the wall; they are voices of the warm dark, of maids, cooks and
gardeners who live in the black world beyond the gates.
Sooner or later the sirens of the police quick-response unit
will ricochet through the dark and the assembled Rottweilers,
Dobermans and German Shepherds will burst into unlovely
barking. Somewhere out there, men will be hurtling towards a
scene of violence and destruction while others struggle to feel
secure inside the boundaries of their homes.

The cacophony beyond my high walls will eventually die
down to be replaced by a rising murmur of voices: Zulu,
Xhosa, Tswana, Sotho, Shangaan, all tongues of the sub-conti-
nent. It is only in the morning that the newspapers may record
the death of some unknown burglar, an unlucky householder
or young policeman killed in a hail of automatic rifle fire. More
statistics for a city with the highest murder rate in the world.

AFRICA

For me, and numerous other inmates of the northern suburbs, the border begins at the front gate: the first of many boundaries that surround each individual in concentric circles of fear and alienation. They are the tracklines of apartheid, running deep and wide through city, town and village.

In a country founded and sustained on the principle of divide and rule, great attention was given to the matter of borders. Armies of Afrikaner bureaucrats were tasked with creating states within states, with legislating division in every area of human existence.

Nothing was spared this policy of separation; the apartheid map-makers drew their stubby pencils through every facet of life. Laws to impose borders where races could and could not live; laws to divide where they could go to school and university; even laws to separate them in the bedroom, in marriage and in death.

The policy of grand apartheid was designed to create separate black states where the different tribes could live in varying degrees of poverty and subjugation while providing a pool of willing labour for the factories and farms of white South Africa. To resolve the matter of the blacks who lived within the borders of the republic there was petty apartheid: that plethora of laws which forbade anything but a master-servant relationship between black and white.

The search for racial purity would later founder on the rocks of reality, but not before the map-makers gave us four so-called independent tribal republics: Transkei, Bophuthatswana, Venda and Ciskei.

Along with these they created black homelands which, theoretically, aspired to nationhood: KwaZulu, KwaNdeble, Qua Qua, KaNgwane, Gazankulu and Lebowa. The world refused to recognize the independence of these so-called states, seeing them as the fictional tools of apartheid. But it did not stop Pretoria from dumping thousands of black South

Africans into make-believe countries they were now supposed to claim as their own.

The clearances and mass removals were implemented with a scientific vengeance: a story of lives uprooted and packed off to the wilderness on the backs of lorries. Within the borders of these states they were free to 'develop' separately, to join the struggle for survival of their impoverished fellow-citizens.

The rulers of the homelands wasted no time in creating for themselves the illusion of sovereignty: police forces, armies, flags and grand parliamentary buildings. But it was all funded by the scientists of apartheid from their laboratories in Pretoria and independence was, of course, a sham.

My first encounter with the realities of life in the homelands occurred nearly ten years ago while I was travelling through the Xhosa homeland of Transkei, at the time labouring under the rule of Kaiser Matanzima. I remember it as a journey through cold hill country where ragged children drifted out of the mist at crossroads begging for money. The housing consisted of little round thatched huts surrounded by tiny plots of overgrazed land. Those inimitable symbols of the homelands, the goats, scavenged by the roadside with a few scrawny cattle.

On countless occasions since then I have crossed the borders of the homelands to be greeted by similar scenes: the actual countryside may differ but the overriding impression of poverty and deprivation rarely does. In the majority of cases you cross the border without even being aware of the fact, save for a small notice at the side of the road.

But one day these homelands will be history, subsumed into the reality of a black-ruled South Africa. The border lines on the map of grand apartheid will disappear, to be replaced by the borders of regions in which black and white will, theoretically, live as equals. I say theoretically because only the most wildly optimistic can imagine the border between privilege and poverty disappearing with majority rule. New regional borders – estimates of regions vary between ten and sixteen – will be based on some concept of reality, not the race-driven insanity of the homeland boundaries. In the cities there are plans for multi-racial councils to rule both township and white suburb. The administrative boundaries between the likes of Alexandra township and the white area of Sandton, both suburbs of Johannesburg, will supposedly disappear.

Yet the asphalt highways that serve as borders between the sprinkled lawns of Sandton and the garbage-strewn and over-crowded streets of Alexandra will remain. The black unemployed who stand on the hills outside Alexandra waiting for work will be able to glimpse the green trees and sparkling pools of the northern suburbs, but they will only ever enter that world as servants or burglars.

The centre of Johannesburg has become less a mixed neighbourhood than a black one. Whites now venture into areas like Hillbrow and Joubert Park with apprehension, fearing the Africaness of streets crowded with people from all over the continent. The voices of Ghana, Zaire and Nigeria now clamour above those of native South Africans.

This in itself is an indication of how the borders between the republic and the black-ruled states of Africa have been relaxed, turning the centre of Johannesburg into an African city quite unlike the strange imitation of Europe and America that existed before. On these streets there is a sense of Africa reclaiming its own. Across town in Yeoville and Berea there is the beginning of a truly multi-racial culture with black, white, coloured and Indian sharing the streets, bars and restaurants with no evident sign of animosity.

Yet it must be remembered that such suburbs are not typical of South Africa and the most impenetrable border of all remains: the barrier created by fear and mistrust. They are learned emotions, the product of upbringing and schooling among the black and white alike. They are the burden of memory and history, separating people in a deeper way than any physical barrier.

The words of poet Shabir Banoobhai seem particularly apposite in this respect:

> The border is as far as the black man
> who walks alongside you
> as secure as your door
> against the unwanted knock

It is only in overcoming this legacy of fear that the true border can be crossed into the country described by the Afrikaans writer André Brink, who spoke of his desire for the 'Freedom, the openness, the open-endedness, the endlessness – of a country for which the future is still possible, a love not yet circumscribed, a story not yet written.'

A SPEAR IN THE BELLY

Ulundi, January 1993

The Inkatha leader Chief Buthelezi was warning of a potential
blood bath in South Africa, a warning prompted by his fear that
the ANC and the government were reaching secret agreements
on the country's future. The Chief delivered his warning at the
battleground of Isandhlwana where a Zulu army crushed a
British invasion force in January 1879.

As we came around the clump of thornbush and elephant
grass the Buffalo River came suddenly into view. It swept
through the darkening valley, swollen with summer rains and
coloured a light brown shade by the upland silt it had
devoured on its winding course through Zululand. In this part
of the valley, steep cliffs rose up on the opposite side of the
riverbank and beyond them we could make out the conical
peak of a mountain, almost shrouded in thick cloud. A storm
was gathering on the plateau beyond the mountain. We could
hear its unsteady pulse punching through the canopy of cloud.

It was at approximately this time of evening in similar
weather conditions that the survivors of the Battle of
Isandhlwana came crashing down the riverbank, pursued by
the spears and the victorious cries of the Zulu army. A few
made it to safety but most were stabbed and hacked where
they stood or they drowned in the flood waters of the Buffalo
River. Beyond them, on the plain below the sphinx-like shape
of the Isandhlwana mountain, the bodies of several thousand
men lay in the last agonies of death. More than 800 imperial
and 400 colonial soldiers and native attendants died. Some
3000 Zulus fell in the advance on the thin red line of the
empire. A young Zulu herdboy who observed the scene said

with stark simplicity, 'We saw the ground and it was red'.

It was a stunning victory for this African army against the battle-hardened troops of the empire. The defeat was to send shock-waves through Britain and precipitate the departure of Disraeli from power and the return of Gladstone and the liberals. But its effects were to be felt long beyond the imperial age, for the Zulu victory was short-lived. The loss of men at the battle and the subsequent British victory at Ulundi saw the end of Zulu power, and the fall of a nation which had conquered and subdued a vast area of present-day South Africa. Ahead lay exile for their King Cetswayo and, beyond that, the humiliation of apartheid: the dismemberment of their state into poverty-stricken enclaves within the homeland system.

Standing in the shadow of Isandhlwana on a blisteringly hot afternoon, listening to Chief Buthelezi, Cetswayo's direct descendant, I pondered the rows of warriors listening to him. They sat motionless on the dusty ground, their shields and spears beside them, listening to their leader warn of another blood bath, like the Anglo-Zulu war.

Later one of them told me he would be willing to do battle for his chief. 'We beat the British and they were a great tribe. We can beat any other nation,' he said. I wanted to remind him that although the Zulus had won the battle they had ultimately lost the war, but in the rising din of chanting warriors I decided that discretion was the better part of valour.

The men who chanted their praise for Chief Buthelezi were, for the most part, poor peasants who lived on some of the most over-grazed and badly eroded land in Southern Africa. The years of white hegemony had left them with little in the material sense, but had accentuated their desire to hold on to a Zulu identity, one that takes pride in military prowess, in the memory of past conquest and the subjugation of other tribes. It is a tradition based on loyalty to the king and his chiefs, in which the will of the individual is bound over to that of the leader. This is something Chief Buthelezi understands. In blunt terms he represents the image of their mighty ancestors and he himself has consciously cultivated this comparison.

To a people robbed of their lands and rights, his evocation of Zulu pride must be irresistible. The ANC with its modernist approach, its talk of a western-style model of democracy, represents a threat to these men. They have witnessed young ANC comrades challenging the control of the chiefs, a challenge that represents an unthinkable threat to the hierarchical system of rural Zulu life.

The response to these challenges has often been bloody, with Zulu battling Zulu, in what Chief Buthelezi calls a low-level civil war. But if it is a war between the old and the new, it is also dominated by the personality of Mangosuthu Buthelezi. Demonized to extraordinary lengths by his opponents, lauded by often sycophantic admirers, he is a complex man who has shown himself capable of both ruthlessness and subtlety. That he does have a considerable body of support is accepted by most realistic observers of the political scene. What is now in question is where exactly he will lead his supporters. Back to negotiations or into a new war in which traditionalist Zulus prepare to fight the forces of a new non-racial government.

The lesson of the last Zulu war must surely be that battle may bring one glorious victory, but in the longer term it leaves the tribe divided and weak or, to paraphrase the words of King Cetswayo, with a spear thrust into its belly.

VOYAGE TO HELL!

Cape Town, February 1993

A fishing trip in the shadow of Table Mountain proved to be
an unforgettable experience.

The fishing party was made up of myself, a Zimbabwean
cameraman, an American magazine correspondent and a BBC
colleague. We all had, I suppose, visions of a day from the
pages of Hemingway, strapped into our seats as fabulous
marlin and tuna hurled themselves into the air struggling to
escape our masterful hold.

All we needed now was the boat. We searched for the craft,
whose description I had been given, but could find no sign of
it on the water. I began to feel the first stirrings of apprehension. And then it appeared, being towed down the road behind
a Land Rover. It was not the grand vessel we had been expecting. No, far from it. In length the boat can have been no more
than twenty-four feet, with a small canopy at the front which
provided some protection from the wind and waves. The window of the Land Rover wound down and a head emerged,
smiling a little uncertainly I thought. 'My name is Louis,' said
the balding head, 'this is Mike.'

At that point a youth with short spiky hair came around
the back of the boat and helped to take our bags on board. We
had brought ample provisions: salads, cold meats, sandwiches,
drinks and beer. The makings of a hearty picnic at sea. As Mike,
the youth, began the process of reversing the trailer down the
slipway, Louis produced a yellow form from his pocket. It
was the usual disclaimer: we promised that whatever might
happen he, Louis, would not be responsible. With a growing
sense of trepidation we signed and climbed aboard.

The water within the harbour wall was glassy and calm and our first few minutes' progress was stately and serene. The captain's dog, a neurotic-looking terrier, nuzzled up against my leg, clinging to me with what I thought a desperate tenacity. Within seconds I learned why. The boat began to rise into the air. 'Hold on, you're going to get wet,' Louis shouted. The waves crashed over the canopy and we clung on for dear life as the boat lurched into the thunder of sea and wind. Suddenly, the glassy calm had become an inky black nightmare. The boat would crash hard into a wave and then sail into the air, suspended for a nerve-wracking second before landing in the water again with a sickening thud.

'Anyone for a beer?' shouted Louis above the din of the engine, waves and wind. We shook our heads frantically in a deranged gesture of refusal. I gazed behind me at the disappearing shore and noticed a family of seals following the boat. Louis saw them too and, swigging from his beer, pointed to a shotgun near his feet. 'I shoot them with that,' he said. 'Aren't they protected?' my American friend managed to gasp as he clung fiercely to the boat rail. 'They might be protected, but if you want to catch a great white shark, they're the best bait you can get,' came the reply.

Louis now reached for a bottle of brandy. 'Anybody like some?' he called again. We were, by now, too speechless with terror to respond. Ten o'clock in the morning and our captain was laying into the beer and brandy.

Beside me, my BBC colleague had turned a ghostly grey colour. He lunged towards the side of the boat and was sick. As he came back to the centre and lay down on his back, Louis approached with one of the greasiest chicken pies I've ever seen. 'Like a pie, John?' he offered. John looked at him with as much loathing as he could muster and groaned aloud. A huge wave crashed over the boat. Most of it seemed to cover John. His eyes began to take on a murderous aspect. I began to fear a mutiny.

There was still no sign of us stopping to fish. 'Seventeen more miles,' promised Louis, who then launched into a diatribe against AIDS victims. 'They should be locked in a building and left to die,' he said. That was only the beginning. 'You know, I'm not a racialist but – ever since Mandela was let out of prison, this country's gone to hell,' he went on and on and on.

This was the ultimate South African nightmare: miles out on a dangerous sea with a raving drunken racist – a chance to get really close to the worst aspects of white South African manhood. It was a combination of macho bravado and blind ignorance. We began to feel sorry for his assistant Mike, and the wretched dog, shivering on the sodden deck. To have to endure this man, day in day out, was as close to hell as could be imagined. The wind was now howling around us, the sky seeming to press into the waves. With almost one voice we shouted, 'Take us home!'

But the journey back was a roller-coaster ride through hell, Louis pushing the boat for every last knot. When, after an eternity, we reached the tranquillity of the harbour and tied up alongside the jetty, Louis produced his visitors' book. We gazed at him in disbelief, like some veterans of a distant pointless war. 'No way am I signing,' my American friend said, pushing his way forward onto the land. Of all of us only my colleague John paused to write, he who had suffered worst of all. I gazed over his shoulder and saw him write the words, 'Never, ever, ever again.'

A CASUAL EXERCISE

Johannesburg, March 1993

As a new South Africa began to emerge from an iniquitous past, three white men went on trial for murder.

The mine dumps of Benoni loom out of the landscape like mountains on some stark lifeless planet. They are the residue of deep burrowing in the earth, the hungering after gold which gives towns like Benoni, and others along the Reef, a reason for existing. This is scrubland on which the mine dumps and the acres of suburban bungalows were imposed, as the Witwatersrand was opened up by the settlers in the closing stages of the last century.

The gold hunger brought with it the need for a large pool of native labour, the people who gaze out at us, like dejected shadows, from contemporary photographs. Today Benoni is circled by the townships which house thousands of black South Africans. You may or may not notice them if you travel as a tourist from Johannesburg to the Kruger National Park, but you will certainly see the mine dumps, which dominate the horizon.

What I am fairly sure of is that Samuel Khanagha saw them one clear, autumn morning, less than a year ago. He was sitting in a car, speeding towards one of the dumps and one has every reason to believe that he was afraid – very afraid. Samuel was sitting between two white men, another drove the car. Two black guards followed. Samuel knew the white men, Johan Van Eyk, Francois Oosthuizen and Hendrick Gerber. They were colleagues at the Johannesburg security company where Samuel was a guard. They were taking him to a disused dump, out of the public eye – a place where a man's screams would be lost in the emptiness of the veld.

The court records do not tell us what was said in the car, so we can only imagine the scene: a black man and three white men; he was accused of stealing the equivalent of £15 000, and they were determined to make him admit it. All three white men were former members of the security forces: two had served in a counter-insurgency unit in Namibia; one was the son of the recently retired Deputy Commissioner of Police.

The car pulled up on waste ground and Samuel was hustled out and tied up. Somebody went back to the car and produced an electric-shock machine and a plastic bag. Lying on the ground, Samuel would have seen this happening: the muscular white men chattering to one another in Afrikaans, setting up the machine and wires with which they planned to extract the truth from him. Somebody tied a rope round Samuel's feet and put the plastic bag over his head; he felt himself being dragged along, and then hoisted on to the branch of a tree.

Within a few minutes, we are told, the interrogation began. One of the white men pulled Samuel's trousers down and placed electrodes on his genitals. The electric shocks started, waves of pain that convulsed his body. Soon Samuel was begging for mercy, but he still refused to admit to the crime. He did not do it, he told his tormentors again and again. The white men were thirsty, so they paused. One of the black guards was sent off for drinks. Among the white men there was laughter and bantering. This was hard work, and the day was warm.

Eventually the drinks arrived and Samuel Khanagha begged for something to cool his thirst. He begged for mercy, but his interrogators laughed. The worst had yet to come. Of the three, only Oosthuizen felt any pang of conscience; he offered Khanagha something to drink. We are not told from the records of the court what the reaction of the two black guards was.

The white men appeared by now to have run out of

patience. They began to place wood and sticks under Samuel's body. Somebody added a match, and soon a fire was blazing under the black man's head. Van Eyk, Oosthuizen and Gerber stood back and watched their victim twist in agony as the fire gathered force. They could hear his screams but no one else could. One of the whites pumped several bullets into the dying black man; another cut off his right hand. This bizarre mutilation was never explained in the subsequent trial. By nightfall, Samuel Khanagha was dead, his body abandoned in the bush, his right hand found on a suburban street in Benoni.

When the case came to an end in court last week, the men were sentenced to periods of ten, fifteen and twenty years for Samuel Khanagha's murder. With good behaviour, they could all be free having served less than half their sentences. Had three black men been accused of murdering a white in so horrific a manner, they would doubtless have been sentenced to death.

People die in brutal attacks every day in South Africa. Nobody, no racial or political group, has a monopoly on the exercise of murder. Whites kill blacks, blacks kill other blacks and whites. Yet there is something about the murder of Samuel Khanagha which stands apart; he died at the hands of men who regarded him as little better than an animal, men who took their time with the killing, who carried it out in front of black witnesses and who never even bothered to cover their tracks. All three men were products of a security system that revelled in the casual exercise of brutality over a black underclass.

The system is being dismantled, but the attitudes remain entrenched. What happened to Samuel Khanagha was not an isolated incident, nor was the leniency of the sentencing untypical. Yet the image of this figure, hanging upside down over a burning fire while others laughed at his pleas for mercy, is a challenge to all of us, correspondents, observers and analysts, who speak glibly about a 'new South Africa'.

AT THE EDGE AGAIN

Johannesburg, April 1993

The tortuous negotiation process was thrown off course by the assassination of one of the African National Congress' most senior figures, Chris Hani. The anger among blacks boiled over into violence – and concerns were expressed that law and order in South Africa was on the verge of collapse.

This is a strange and frightening hour in South Africa: the voices of reason are being drowned, swept away in a wave of anger and bitterness. For the first time in my experience, naked hatred of whites is in the eyes and speech of those I meet on township streets. I experienced it myself in Soweto yesterday. An angry crowd surged around my car and chanted the slogan of the radical left, 'One settler, one bullet'. It wasn't much use explaining that as a foreign correspondent I was anything but a colonial settler. This was a crowd seething with hatred and only my black colleague's calming voice soothed them.

A few minutes later, we were swept along to the fence of Protea police station, the township's biggest security base. And then the chaos erupted. I was standing by a wall when a volley of gunfire cut a scythe through the crowd. In their attempts to flee the shooting, they pushed me back over the wall, probably saving me from serious injury. Tear gas enveloped the area and I ran with the surging thousands to the safety of a nearby community hall. Behind me, my BBC colleagues – cameraman Glenn Middleton and soundman Lee Edwards – were lying wounded on the ground.

They were among the 250 people hit by gunfire. They are now thankfully safe, having had several shotgun pellets removed from their bodies. Others were not so lucky: at least three people were killed and many others sustained critical injuries. This was a police response which far exceeded the degree of provocation offered.

At Soweto's giant Baragwanath hospital, I watched the injured being carried in by the dozen. Inside the emergency ward, doctors and nurses struggled to cope with the numbers. The cries and groans of the injured could be heard above the din of ambulances sweeping into the courtyard. Most poignant of all was the face of a woman who watched her husband slip into death and then cried out, 'What for? What for?'

But if the police acted with stupidity in Soweto, one also has to concede that the ANC was patently unable to control its supporters in many areas. The visions of looting and wanton destruction on the streets of Cape Town and Port Elizabeth will linger long in the mind. So, too, will the vision of Nelson Mandela fighting to be heard above the angry shouts of the crowd in Soweto's Jabulani stadium. One could only feel sorry for this gentle and dignified man as he was shouted down by a generation which wants revolution, and not the subtle compromise which Mandela and other ANC leaders advocate. The situation is complicated by the actions of South Africa's huge criminal community, ever eager to ply their trade under the guise of political protest.

As I write, President de Klerk is announcing the deployment of thousands more troops and police, warning of sweeping security measures to contain the unrest. It is a predictable measure, but it will do nothing to diffuse the anger on the streets. For, in essence, what we are witnessing is the rebellion of a lost generation which feels it has waited too long for the freedom and democracy Nelson Mandela promised when he walked free from the gates of Victor Verster prison three years ago.

In the chaos of these past few days, one almost forgets the chilling facts of Chris Hani's murder and the terrible loss he represents, not just to the ANC but to the cause of sanity and reason. It took only seconds for his killer to strike. One moment Chris Hani was stepping out of his car, the next he was dead. In such a manner was the destiny of a great political figure decided and the future of South Africa placed in question.

I have witnessed a previous emergency, that of 1986 when South Africa again seemed to hover on the abyss. Because the situation was brought under control then I am reluctant to predict a complete collapse of law and order. It has always appeared to me that South Africa is the land of the almost apocalypse. Too often in the past, journalists have predicted the imminent demise of the government or a racial blood bath. For that reason you will forgive me if I refuse to make any predictions beyond the sad certainty that the sound of gunfire will fill the air for some time to come.

IVORY PARK

Johannesburg, July 1993

Another squatter camp was destroyed by the authorities as politicians debated the shape of the new South Africa and right-wingers continued to flex their muscles.

We walked up the hill, the smoke from the open coal fires churning in our lungs. Sitting in the dry grass at the side of the road was a group of women and small children, their belongings spread out around them. I and a white colleague approached them to talk, but the children became hysterical. Embarrassed, I backed off. One of the women broke away from the group and explained very simply what had happened. 'You're white, and all this week the white men have been pulling down our shacks. The children cry whenever they see a white man,' she said. I have never quite figured out how to feel in such a situation. There is the rationalization that this has nothing to do with any fault of mine, but somehow that cannot override the old shame of my race.

This incident took place in the Ivory Park squatter camp outside Johannesburg. All week the bulldozers have been at work smashing the flimsy shacks which belong to several hundred black families. This land is required for industrial use according to the bureaucrats of the Transvaal Provincial Administration. Emily Masheko has been sleeping with her five children under a covering of plastic bags and sticks. 'All I want is to live in a house,' she says, 'like the white people. I feel shamed that my children must live like this.' I watched as she bedded the young ones down, five of them and herself under a single blanket in the middle of the South African winter.

During the day, Emily digs a hole in the ground into which

she places her plastic home; this hides it from the bulldozers and their zealous drivers. They have already taken the corrugated iron which formed her original home. The days are spent hiding out in the long grass huddled together around small fires, always watching for the bulldozers. Nearby, another woman, much older, perhaps in her seventies, was trying to erect a plastic shelter. She spent about an hour trying to pound a wooden stake into the ground. When, after much effort, it seemed to be secure, she walked away to fetch the plastic. A small breeze blew up and sent the pole tumbling to the ground. The old woman came back and began again.

A man called Justice came over and introduced himself. When he began to speak, I thought he was suffering from a stutter, but it soon became clear that his lips were trembling with anger: 'We are suffering, my friend. We have no houses, jobs or education. Even the white people's dogs live better than us. They build little houses for their dogs but nothing for us.' It is no comfort to Justice to know that he is one of seven million or so people who are without homes in this new South Africa.

The irony is that this wretched place is only a few miles away from the multi-party negotiations forum at Kempton Park, the place invaded by thousands of right-wingers last week. I had intended writing about them, about how they smashed property and urinated on carpets, insulted black women and attacked any black who got in their way. But, set against the desolation of Ivory Park, the over-dressed thugs of the AWB can wait for another day, save but to wonder how such people would fare living rough and scratching for a living.

It is hard to imagine Mr Terre' Blanche, with his well-fed body, his farm and his comfortable home, shivering in the veld under a piece of plastic. Yet in a curious sense there is a thread which binds Terre' Blanche to Emily and Justice and the other lost souls of the squatter camps. They are all creations of apartheid. The AWB leader's blind bigotry and the squatters' misery come from the same immoral tangle of laws, the same warped philosophy. And as they struggle to shape a new country, the negotiators will know that defeating the racist Right will only be one small step on the road.

The greater challenge, almost overwhelming in its implications, will be in building a South Africa in which there are houses, jobs and schools for those who were systematically denied under apartheid. The new leaders must by now know that out there, beyond the walls of the negotiating chamber, in the scores of squatter camps, people are watching, waiting, hoping for a South Africa in which black children do not automatically become hysterical on the approach of a white man.

SHEPARD'S FUNERAL

Mabopane, August 1993

Black township violence claimed more than 17 000 lives
in the years leading up to South Africa's historic election
of 1994. Often, hundreds of people would be killed
each month. Few were untouched by the violence.

Death came to my personal world this week. It took away
Shepard Gopi in a matter of seconds. He was a gentle human
being whom I knew mostly as a husky voice floating in the
warm darkness of my backyard. Shepard was the boyfriend of
Paulina, an equally gentle person, who has worked for the BBC
for some ten years. He had a job in a large furniture store, had
his own car and seemed to all of us to be a happy man, a man
who looked to the future. He divided his time between my
house and that of a friend in nearby Alexandra township.
When I returned home last Friday night, I found Paulina
sitting at the kitchen table weeping, my wife doing what she
could to offer consolation.

The facts, as explained to me, were brutally simple: the
previous night Shepard had gone to Alexandra to meet
his friend. They went to a drinking club and talked for
several hours. When Shepard came out, a group of gunmen
surrounded him. One of the gang opened fire with an automatic rifle and shot Shepard ten times. On a street where the
rubbish is piled in mounds, Shepard Gopi, Shepard of the
laughing voice, died in a pool of his own blood. The following
day his father arrived at my house, carrying his son's clothes
and a few other personal belongings. This was how Paulina
learned of her lover's death.

As she sat weeping at the kitchen table I felt at a loss as to what to say, how to console her. But Paulina knew, far better than I, that this was death without sense, without reason, without meaning. 'These are terrible times. Why are we killing each other?' she asked. The answer, of course, was one that most people wanted to shy away from, a truth that lurked in the darkness. It lay in recognizing that the humanity had drained out of a great many people, that for the young men who killed Shepard it was as easy to take his life away as it would have been to allow him to live.

The generation that produced Shepard's killers had grown up believing that violence should be their first resort. They had good 'teachers': policemen who shot first and asked questions later, secret police who tortured and murdered with impunity, and distant political leaders who urged them to make their townships ungovernable, their schools into places of revolution. But while the grown-ups have decided it is time to talk, the generation they have spawned have begun to lose themselves in fields of blood. I have encountered such wild-eyed young men on the streets of the townships time and time again in the past month.

They are the people who place burning tyres around the necks of their victims, they make up the gangs that enforce school boycotts and strikes, they are the people who have, of late, taken to digging up the corpses of their enemies and setting them alight. This final act of desecration encapsulates the brutalization, the nihilism which is eating its way into the social fabric of those townships where violence has become endemic.

Before I lose myself in despair, let me return to the short life of Shepard, or more particularly to his funeral. With four of Paulina's friends packed into the car we set off early for the black homeland of Bophutatswana, to the township of Mabopane where the funeral was to take place.

It was a bright, warm morning, and the journey north took us barely forty minutes. This was a township quite different from the ones I had spent so much time in recently. There was order and quiet, with no barricades and no prowling armoured vehicles. We followed a long line of buses and cars to the dusty graveyard, which rose out of the bush about a mile from the township. At the graveside, the family congregated under an awning which had been specially erected. Behind them were singers from one of the burial societies to which township residents pay a sum each month to secure a decent funeral for family members.

The wind came up from the east and sent clouds of dust from the open grave drifting over the mourners. We coughed and turned our faces away. Some women began to sing a lament, one of those old cries of pain that seem to rise out of the ground and fill every pocket of space. One by one we walked to the grave and took a handful of earth, which we cast down on to the coffin of poor dead Shepard.

A notice handed around to mourners noted that he had been born in 1961, and shot dead thirty-two years later. As the diggers began to shovel earth down into the grave, I wept for Shepard and his family and for Paulina, but also for the burned and mutilated dead who had crowded my dreams after the last terrible month in the townships. As we walked away from the graveyard, the minister who had performed the burial service came up to me. 'Thank you for coming,' he said, 'thank you so much. You see,' he said, 'it is that love that is important.'

Standing amid the streams of mourners, I held on to his words: knowing that, in their simplicity, they spoke volumes about this country's amazing capacity for hope in the face of fear, brutality and so much loss.

LETTER FROM LOUIS TRICHARDT

August 1993

Afrikaners were becoming aware that blacks would gradually take control of the settlements they had created to preserve their white culture and traditions.

I crossed the Tropic of Capricorn on an afternoon heavy with the promise of the first rains. Clouds crashed and tumbled far above so that all around the Bushveld took on a morbid grey colour. The mopane trees and thornbush clung to a land that was baked and parched. The long dry scars of riverbeds appeared, the story of the drought years carved into the earth. Only far to the west could I see the glimmerings of light edging out from behind the great masses of cloud. There were mountains there, strange volcanic shapes which hugged the horizon and beyond them, I knew, the vast arid plains of Botswana.

I stopped the car and stood for a few moments at the foot of a granite hill which rose up from the roadside. It was of improbable construction, boulder piled upon boulder with the dark mouths of caves beckoning in its upper reaches.

The landscape of the north is full of such curiosities, hills and small mountains, composed entirely of boulders, lying where they tumbled in the lost days of the volcanic age. This land, which rolled beyond the invisible line of the tropic, was tamer in appearance now than it must have been when the wagons of the first Voortrekkers rolled and groaned forward in the early months of 1835. The lions and leopards, the buffalo and elephant which roamed here were gone, safe now only in the confines of the game reserves. And the Bush itself, though still vast and beautiful, had surely been of wilder appearance. No fences then, no telephone poles, not even the solitary wisps of smoke from distant farmhouses.

Standing by the road I began to think of the old escapists with their bibles and their guns, their blind moral certainty and acute desire to be free of the civilized corruptions of the British empire. And so for a few moments I waited in the savannah and closed my eyes on this evening of early rain. There in the emptiness it was possible to imagine the creaking wagons, to hear the rough cries in Dutch as the cattle were urged forward and to smell the Voortrekkers' scent of oxen and woodsmoke and rough tobacco. It was, to me, as if the whispers of history had hidden in the spaces of the wind, waiting for the solitary traveller to happen along and give himself over to their old call.

The Trekkers had come this way under the leadership of a man named Louis Trichardt. Of him we know comparatively little, other than that he came from the Eastern Cape where the British had placed a price on his head for treason. In the official histories he is known as the man who established European settlements in the far north of South Africa. A man of courage and perseverance.

There is one photograph of Louis Trichardt. The face is that of the Boer patriarch, solemn, stern and dependable. His party of Trekkers comprised, in his own words, seven households and forty-six souls and only nine able shots. They left the Cape in search of a land where they could be free from the interfering British. To men like Louis Trichardt the British were at best meddlesome, at worst treacherous and malign. They taxed the Boers but still expected them to provide men and horses for raids against native tribes. The British themselves dealt mercilessly with native rebellions yet forbade the Afrikaners from owning slaves, and were even prepared to see farmers being taken to court by their servants on charges of ill-treatment.

These, however, were secondary causes when compared to

the growing fear that, unless they quit the Cape, they would lose their identity. This precious sense of a people alone and special before God was still in its genesis among the Boers of the Cape. In the years to come it would prove the most powerful driving force in Afrikaner history.

Back in the early 1830s the close proximity of black families, who were absorbing the traditions and culture of the whites, filled the Boers with anxiety. They felt themselves confronted by a vision of cultural annihilation at the hands of the combined forces of British imperialism and black numbers. The salvation of the volk became the imperative.

I had not long arrived in the town of Louis Trichardt before that same imperative was being preached to me with deadly seriousness. It lies at the foot of the Soutpansberg Mountains whose forested slopes rise to 5000 feet above sea level. These mountains once formed the natural barrier between white settlement and the wild lands of the native tribes beyond. They were, to all intents and purposes, the wall of the siege, inside whose protection the descendants of Trichardt and the other Voortrekkers were to construct the mighty and all-embracing edifice of apartheid.

It is a pretty enough town, though blessed more by its physical situation than by the dull blocks of buildings which make up its core. Beyond the square grid of the business centre the white suburbs ramble pleasingly towards the mountain. They are verdant and thick with flowers: bougainvillaea, flamboyant flame lilies that infuse the air with the heady scent of the tropics.

Lying under the mountain, these suburbs benefit from above-average rainfall and when the rain is poor the sprinklers cast shower after shower on to the well-trimmed lawns. But it is not all so pretty or privileged. The houses of the poor whites, victims of recession and sanctions, have the sad air of places that once knew plenty but are now slowly succumbing to the combined effects of poverty and broken pride.

I have met many of these people at meetings of groups like the AWB. They seem irredeemably lost and bitter; they who have watched the dream of apartheid with its Job Reservation and Group Areas Acts evaporate before their dazed eyes. Now, on the streets of Louis Trichardt, they see a town that is slowly becoming African. The self-conscious Europeanness, the order and neatness are slowly giving way to an older reality. The laughter and bustle and chaos of black Africa is edging up the main street. This year it may be streaming noisily around the food and clothes shops at the end of Trichardt and Crock Streets, but some day soon those watching know that this will be a black town.

When the Trekkers settled in this district they used their guns to deal with the black tribes, yet in time they were corrupted by the easy access to black labour and the cycle of mutual dependency began. Now in numerous farm towns like Louis Trichardt, men like Koeks Terblanche talk of starting over again. Like his more notorious namesake Koeks is a believer in old-style apartheid. Hendrik Verwoerd, with his legions of police inspecting people's beds and underwear for evidence of inter-racial sex, was Koeks' kind of man. I met him in the offices of the Conservative Party.

Koeks grew up a nationalist, a devout follower of D.F. Malan and Verwoerd. On his farm he knew how to keep the blacks in their place. 'I just gave them a hiding if they got cheeky,' he told me. He also believes that the early Trekkers like Louis Trichardt prayed too much and shot too little, pointing to the treatment of the American Indians or the Australian Aborigines as laudable attempts at population control.

Koeks wears a gun these days and told me there would be a war unless he and the Conservative majority of whites in Louis Trichardt were given a white homeland where they could rule themselves. 'Where might that be?' I asked, knowing that the great empty spaces which enabled the first trek to take place had all disappeared. 'That is the problem,' replied Koeks, who thought that allocating the northern and western Transvaal and part of the Orange Free State might be a good start. 'I don't hate every black, there are some good blacks, it's just the majority I have a problem with,' he added.

Like most right-wingers Koeks was notable for his lack of guile. He had the capacity to say things that were outrageously racist without the veneer of pseudo-science, the talk of group rights and cultural differences, which until recently was the vogue with President de Klerk and his advisors.

Before I left, Koeks assured me that right-wingers were not bluffing, they would fight. Three of his neighbours have died at the hands of marauding gangs in recent months, among them a woman forced to drink caustic soda. To a man reared inside a psychological stockade such acts were evidence of the malign force, the conspiracy of black barbarians and white traitors waiting to devour his tribe. I left him with a hand-shake, feeling I had probably heard the strongest threats the right-wingers of Louis Trichardt had to offer. But I was wrong, sadly and completely wrong.

About ten miles from the town there is a museum based on the site of the original Trekker settlement. Here they have recreated the mud cottages of the Trichardt era. There are ancient ox-wagons and old Dutch bibles which were excavated at the scene. My guide introduced himself as Ferdi. He was an amiable giant of a man who went out of his way to show me around.

At the end, I asked him the inevitable question of these days: what did he think of the way things were going? At this, the genial guide became the angry demagogue. 'Look here,' he said, pulling up his shirt and showing two great purple stripes on his skin, 'that is where I was shot and blown up on the border.'

He had been in the élite reconnaissance unit of the army operating deep inside Angola in a war that claimed the life of his brother. Being wounded meant a limp for life and the end of his military career. After that, there was just freelance security work and that was what brought him here as supervisor to a team of black guards. 'I hate the blacks, I hate the kaffirs,' he exploded.

Ferdi told me that his child had been kidnapped by black robbers and rescued by police. The experience had left him distraught. He assured me that, if he could, he would kill Nelson Mandela. Then he regained his composure, smiled and handed me a pamphlet on the history of the Voortrekkers. Unlike Koeks Terblanche and his white homeland, Ferdi planned to stay just where he was and fight it out.

I was, by now, somewhat doom-laden with talk of war and even if Ferdi's feelings were the result of a blinding personal tragedy, I could not escape their racist expression.

Driving back to Louis Trichardt I experienced one of the darkest moods of my time in South Africa so far. Coming into the town through the thick bush country I noticed the spire of the Dutch reform church, rising high above the shops and banks and civic offices. Here, if anywhere, I thought, I will find the moderate voice. For once on this journey I was correct. Dominee Gerhard Botha showed me into his study with an offer of coffee and an assurance that he had plenty of time to talk.

As he prepared the coffee in another room I noticed photographs of the young minister in an army uniform; an old artillery shell was standing next to a bookcase full of theological works and wholesome historical novels. Above the books were two photographs, one of a dark-haired young woman and beside that a portrait of two young children, both blonde like their father.

When he sat down, I asked him bluntly if the town was as completely conservative as I imagined. 'Oh, it's not only conservative, I would say very AWB,' he said, with a smile. Over the course of the next hour he described how he walked a tightrope in his sermons: preaching social justice and equality but carefully avoiding party politics.

He spoke of the cult of violence and the problems of alcohol and wife-beating which were coming to the fore in his community; of the fear which gripped so many Afrikaners, fear of the blacks but also fear of themselves, of whether in spite of their rhetoric they had it in themselves to survive the future.

Dominee Gerhard Botha believes in a new country with justice for all. Somewhere down the line he could even see his own descendants inter-marrying with blacks. For a man raised in a community so obsessed with the need for group cohesion, the willingness to even contemplate such a possibility was to me at any rate evidence of a trek begun away from the stultifying prejudices of the apartheid era.

Don't get me wrong, Dominee Gerhart Botha was no liberal in the Western sense of the word. His personal mores were conservative and he has traditional views about the duty to God and country. It is his definition of country that makes him different. It is not the place of ultimate escape envisioned by Louis Trichardt and his Trekkers, neither is it the white homeland demanded by Koeks Terblanche, or least of all Ferdi's place of war. No, it is a new unknown country where the colour of a man's skin ceases to be the definition of his worth.

Before I could leave, there was one question which had to be asked. 'Tell me,' I said, 'do you believe the right-wingers when they say they'll go to war?' Perhaps because he had been so positive earlier, I was somewhat taken aback by the reply, 'I would believe them,' he said, but added as I walked away, 'don't forget the majority of Afrikaners want peace.'

Driving away from Louis Trichardt through the emptiness of twilight, no other car for miles, I struggled to know which of the voices of the disappearing town I should heed. Those

which promised war or the sane voice of peace and reconciliation. But in the gathering dark in this country of unquiet
ghosts I could find no answer, no certainty. The words from the
pen of André Brink, the celebrated Afrikaans novelist, came to
mind: 'Such a long journey ahead,' he wrote, 'not a question of
imagination but of faith.'

THE CHICKEN FARM

Johannesburg, October 1993

Not all of South Africa's black children supported school boycotts
and attended demonstrations. Some believed education and
self-help provided a more positive path to change.

It is mid-winter and a dry cold wind is gathering the dust into
clouds that sweep over the desolate acres of the veld. In the
midst of the dust I can make out the shape of a building. From
a distance it looks small, insignificant, but, as we approach, the
outline of a much larger structure becomes apparent.

Rattling over the bone-dry ground, we swerve to avoid
boulders and crevices and the huge mounds of rubbish loom-
ing out of the brown dust clouds. Eventually we arrive at the
gates of the Chicken Farm School; row upon row of long concrete bunkers that once housed thousands of chickens being
fattened for the dinner tables of Johannesburg. These former
chicken coops now house 9000 children and ninety-two
teachers. By any reckoning that must make Chicken Farm one
of the largest schools in the world, catering for infants,
primary and secondary level pupils.

As I wait for the headmaster, Peter Kekana, I notice an air
of calm that seems distinctly out of place considering the war-
torn image of black schools of the 1990s. Looking out of the
office window, I see groups of pupils strolling peacefully to
class and in the distance there is the sound of mathematics
tables being recited. A quick scan of the nearby walls reveals
not a single liberation slogan, no sign of the familiar 'One
Settler, One Bullet' or 'Viva ANC'.

Kekana arrives within minutes, a thin, slightly stooped
man who exudes gentleness and warmth. He has been the

headmaster of the secondary school since it was founded by black parents and teachers three years ago. His own story is one of struggle and personal growth. He was one of the leaders of the student rebellion of 1976, a militant who 'burned a few schools down' and spent time in the custody of the security police before fleeing to neighbouring Botswana.

Although Kekana suffered for his political beliefs, he is determined not to be infected with bitterness. He has matured, grown up and warns against bitterness and a belief in violence being passed on to children. For this reason the use of corporal punishment is outlawed in the school. The emphasis is on mutual respect and on looking to the future. 'It is all based on the principle of loving the kid. We believe that if you do that the kid is going to give love in return. If you teach the kid violence, he is going to become violent,' says Kekana.

In an area which has seen hundreds of deaths such words have a particular significance. Many of the children attending Chicken Farm School have been forced to leave schools in the townships because of the level of violence. What they find is an atmosphere far removed from the stress and danger of the classrooms they left behind. This, according to Kekana, is the last chance for many of the children. 'I look at it always in the context of what I experienced,' he says. 'The school boycotts, the demonstrations, the police raids - all that kind of thing which disrupted normal schooling. I know that I would have been a much better person today if it were not for that. That hurts me and I am not going to allow it to happen to these kids.'

Because of his determination to keep politics out of school Kekana does not allow his pupils to take part in strikes and boycotts. He is vehemently opposed to the slogan 'Liberation before education'. That is not to say the children, who range in age from three to sixteen years, do not have strong political views. They certainly do. The difference is that their awareness is being channelled into constructive debate and not into the nihilistic demonstrations that have paralysed black education elsewhere in the country.

I recall one recent visit to a large secondary school in Soweto. The headmaster seemed to have reached the end of his tether. Everywhere one looked there were symptoms of disintegration: smashed windows, broken furniture and the rank smell of urine. The majority of pupils did not come to school. Those that did were roughly divided into two categories: the predators who enforced their will using spurious political justification, and the victims, who were tormented and coerced.

One ten-year-old in the latter category told of endless bullying by self-appointed commissars. 'When they say you stay at home, you stay. Otherwise they call you a sell-out,' he said. And being labelled a 'sell-out' in the tinderbox atmosphere of the townships can amount to a death sentence. Add to that the legacy of apartheid discrimination in education, and you have a child with only minimal hopes of rising above the misery of the ghetto.

The contrast with Chicken Farm could not be greater. Yes, there are severe financial problems, but the principle of self-help is being applied in an effort to overcome these. As I walked around the school with Kekana he pointed to the long rows of concrete classrooms. 'These used to be chicken coops, but the children rebuilt them. They are damn proud of it, I can tell you,' he comments.

The state would not provide desks and seats. So the teachers and children begged a local transport company to donate their old bus seats. The result is row upon row of children perched on bus seats, their text books folded on their knees. The message pushed home every day is simple and, to politically conscious youth, attractive: do not wait for the white man to give you everything, do it for yourself.

Marcelina Mofokeng, who teaches English to secondary

pupils, has come as a volunteer. Her salary is a pittance but she says she is motivated by the desire to end the educational oppression of black children. 'They are the community of tomorrow. Where will we be if they cannot even read and write?' she asks.

Sitting in the class of shy eleven and twelve-year-olds is Sipho Xaba. He is the child of squatter parents who live in a shack about one mile from the school. His preoccupation, however, is not with the marginal circumstances of the present but with his hope for the future.

'I want to be a reporter like you. That is why I am here,' he announces with beaming self-confidence. I, for one, will not be too surprised if the by-line of Sipho Xaba is proudly emblazoned on some newspaper, or if he is heard introducing a broadcast news report, in the not too distant future. As a dedicated partner in South Africa's bravest educational experiment, young Sipho has at least got a fighting chance.

DOMINGO AND JUSTE

Menongue, Angola, November 1993

As the two sides in Angola's civil war continued to do battle,
aid and medical workers struggled against impossible odds to
maintain some shred of humanity.

As we came in from the air, the landscape seemed to hover in
the heat, a watercolour upon whose fluid canvas we could
make out the shapes of buildings and roads, set against an
immensity of shimmering brown bushland. It was possible
from several thousand feet to detect in this vision a sense of the
peaceful and normal. Armies and guns did not want to exist in
the world which spread out from our vantage point among the
clouds. And then the plane began to corkscrew. For those not
initiated in the pleasures of evasive flying, the corkscrew
manoeuvre involves circling sharply down to land. It is a tactic
which offers some protection against surface-to-air missiles,
but little against the bullets of wild gunmen who spray into
the air as planes come in to land.

The two pilots were Americans, veterans of the flying
world, too old to fly at home, but perfectly entitled to ferry
food to Angola's siege towns. They were the kind of grizzled,
no-nonsense men among whom one felt safe from the dan-
gers of war. As we taxied along the runway, I saw the wreck-
age of a MiG fighter, and a larger transport plane, scattered
along the verge. The barrels of anti-aircraft guns poked out
from the high grass and soldiers lounged about in front of
the dilapidated terminal. To describe it as a terminal is perhaps overstating the case. There were several empty dirty
rooms, a store for food and the rather neater quarters of the
commanding officer.

In the arrivals room a policewoman bustled about taking the details of our passports and insisting that we fill in visa forms. We might have been in Angola, but the town of Menongue, it seemed, was a place apart, a place for which special permission was needed. The Portuguese used to call it the place at the end of the world, a fond description for one of the sleepier and more remote corners of the colonial empire. Now, in the time of war and hunger, the description evoked a sense of the sinister and dark.

Driving into town with the Red Cross I had the feeling I always get when arriving in places where evil things have happened. It is a sensation which lies somewhere between deep apprehension and outright fear. The scene which we had observed from the air was indeed a mirage, for the town was ruined. The handsome buildings of the Portuguese had been shelled into piles of rubble. Red terracotta tiles lay strewn across the roads like broken crockery. The façade of the Hotel de Sol was peppered with the marks of heavy machine-gun fire. Nothing had been spared the shooting and bombardment, save for a few jacaranda trees whose glorious purple flowers went sailing down the main street in the breeze.

That afternoon we visited the hospital, another place of weeping, where the wounded, the dying and the displaced lay packed together in dirty wards. So many images gathered in a single visit: the child dying from cerebral malaria, quiet as his life faded away, the soldier with half a face, and the brothers, Domingo and Juste.

All day long, Domingo, aged seven, carried Juste, aged two, to the toilet on his back. In the painful, innocent language of the young, Domingo said, 'He was nice before, but now he has the hunger'. The smaller child could hear me but he looked out from eyes which were lost behind deep dark clouds. This was the result of malnutrition, the steady loss of bodily functions which had condemned a two-year-old to the terrifying world of the sightless. A Canadian aid worker thought the boy was in an advanced stage of malnutrition and that he might die.

It is now several weeks later. I do not know if poor blind Juste died. I could not carry him with me as his brother carried him. I did not know how to save his life and he was one among many of Angola's lost children. But I am left with this feeling of hopelessness and guilt. I filmed this child and recorded his cries, and am told that some people were awakened to the horrors of Angola because of this. Why then this emptiness, this searching? Perhaps because I was leaving for a safer place, carrying the image of their suffering while they lingered behind on the edge of death. Perhaps, too, because I was being faced with the harsh truths: that in Angola man's cruelty was outpacing his humanity; that war-mangled life was leaving the courageous doctors, nurses and aid workers to do what they could against impossible odds.

As I waited for the plane out, sitting among the wounded and the refugees in the stifling hot terminal, I leafed through one of the slim volumes of poetry I always carry with me on journeys. There in the collected works of the Russian poetess, Anna Akhmatova, I found a poem entitled 'The First Long Range Artillery Shell in Leningrad'. I will conclude by quoting some lines because they seem so terribly apt.

> This wasn't a normal city sound,
> it came from unfamiliar country.
> And my distracted hearing would
> not believe it, if only because of
> the wild way it started, grew and
> caught, and how indifferently it
> brought death to my child.

LAST DAYS OF THE EMPIRE

Cape Town, December 1993

South Africa's first non-racial constitution was finally voted into law, bringing to an end 350 years of white domination in the country. It was also the end of the minority-rule parliament.

It is Christmas in Cape Town in the last days of the white empire and the party is in full swing. The streets are crammed with shoppers and the beaches crowded with glistening bodies. Outside the temperature is a pleasant thirty degrees centigrade, the heat not too oppressive thanks to the strong breezes which rush in from the Atlantic, scattering hats and scooping parasols out of the hands of old women as they wander along the promenade at Sea Point.

It is as if all the tension and fear of the past year have been suspended for one last great spree before the arrival of black rule with its myriad uncertainties. The bars and restaurants of the city's new Waterfront complex are crammed, talk of politics is politely discouraged. From a seat at one of the outdoor cafés you can gaze up at Table Mountain where the drifts of thick cloud roll over the summit and down towards the forests of bluegum trees, almost to the back gardens of the princely houses on the lower slopes.

All this week white parliamentarians have been enjoying these views, many of them knowing that it is the last time they will be doing so at the taxpayers' expense. Inside the building, with its cool marbled corridors and leather benches, with its hints of Westminster and gentlemen's clubs, there is an atmosphere akin to the final week at school before the students leave to face the challenges and pitfalls of the future. MPs have spent the last days packing up their books and files, some having decided to retire, others hoping against hope that they'll be returned after next April's all-race election.

From the back benches the future looks anything but rosy. The latest polls give the National Party around twenty per cent of the vote, a figure which, if translated into seats in parliament, would mean that a large proportion of the sitting MPs would have to find other careers. And yet it is a view more pleasant by far than that from the other side of Table Mountain. For there, on acres of dusty scrubland, are the South African majority, crammed into box-like houses of one or two rooms, sheltering under the tin roofs of shanty towns or, in many cases, struggling to wrap pieces of old plastic over branches so that a rough tent-like structure is created. You can see them on your way to and from the soon-to-be-renamed D.F. Malan airport - a grey smear of shacks along the side of the road, a world the white passer-by enters at his or her peril.

There are high watchtowers situated at strategic points along the highway. This is the consequence of several stone-throwing attacks on white motorists. Soldiers now watch over the sullen inmates of Guguletu, Crossroads and Kayelitshe, their automatic weapons a warning to any youths who might think of hurling a projectile at the tourists flocking to the beaches and wine lands of the Cape.

This non-white majority has been denied political rights and human dignity throughout the three-and-a-half centuries of white hegemony in South Africa. For them the parliament, with its pomp-filled official opening, its black-robed speaker and be-medalled state president, was the place where the misery of apartheid was constructed. All the laws of separation were promulgated and debated here - white voices discussing the ruin of non-white lives. The man regarded as the true architect of apartheid, Hendrick Verwoerd, was assassinated in the same chamber, stabbed to death by a deranged messenger who said that a tapeworm had told him to kill the Prime Minister.

There were lone voices of protest, like that of Mrs Helen Suzman, who used the parliamentary system to expose the lies and hypocrisy of successive governments. Other liberals followed in her wake, but there were no black voices to be heard, ever. They could enter this world only as servants, never as the political equals of the white overlords.

In a few years' time, people may well look back and shake their heads in amazement at the fact that, in the later part of the twentieth century, a country existed where men and women were denied the right to vote because of the colour of their skin. That country is fast disappearing. The mockery of democracy which the parliament represented is fast becoming a memory while the new lords of the future prepare to take over.

The new lords were in parliament this week. Watching from the public gallery was the ANC's Cyril Ramaphosa. Other members of his organization were being taken on tours of the building, some doubtless eyeing up the offices they would be occupying after next April. In the end, the parliament which the ANC once wanted to storm has been taken over by persuasion, and one detects a feeling of disbelief among many of the white MPs as they gather their belongings and head out into the bright sunshine and uncertain future.

THE NATURE OF RACISM

Stellenbosch, February 1994

It wasn't only blacks who joined the African National Congress. The party also attracted at least one name more usually associated with South Africa's apartheid history.

The young man paused in the middle of a sentence to wave at a black friend who was passing along the street. They exchanged a few words of warm greeting before he returned to his lengthy polemic about the nature of racism and the need to rebuild completely South African society. This young man had a long angular face framed by thin wisps of blond hair. His voice was quiet and steady, lacking all dogmatism and seeking to convince by the steady drip of reason.

We had met a few minutes earlier in the suffocating midday heat of a high summer day in the university town of Stellenbosch. The blinding white light of the sun was invading every corner of the street, which was quickly emptying of people and animals. All were seeking the precious shade of shops and houses and the few trees which rose through breaks in the concrete.

The young man I had come to interview seemed oblivious to the immobilizing effects of the heat. He continued talking, speaking of a new nation which would be neither white, black nor brown, but South African first and last. In a country which has had a long tradition of English-speaking liberalism, such views ought not to surprise. But when they are articulated by a man bearing the name Verwoerd the listener perks up and pays attention.

Wilhelm Verwoerd is the grandson of Hendrick Frensch Verwoerd, rigid enforcer of racial separation, the man known as apartheid's most ardent disciple. H.F. Verwoerd of the steely blue eyes and blind certainty had meant to create in South

Africa a white state which would last for centuries. It was he, after all, who had said that there was no place for the African in European society above the levels of certain forms of labour.

Now, in the town where H.F. Verwoerd had been a professor, the town which had been the intellectual cradle of apartheid, his grandson was proudly explaining to me why he had joined the African National Congress. Wilhelm Verwoerd is an Afrikaner who has chosen to confront and attempt to destroy the stereotypical image of his tribe. This is the image which portrays the Afrikaner as a pot-bellied, bearded racist in khaki who spends his time telling international television crews that he is preparing for a war against black domination.

Not that the task has been easy for this principled young man. His father refuses to speak to him, believing he has betrayed Afrikanerdom. When a journalist recently rang Professor Wilhelm Verwoerd Senior at Stellenbosch University asking for his son's telephone number, he was told, 'I do not have it, and if I did I would not give it to you'. In a recent letter to the Cape Afrikaans newspaper *Die Burger*, Professor Verwoerd said that no self-respecting Afrikaner would join the ANC.

Wilhelm Verwoerd grew up in a home where the traditional image of blacks as childlike, irresponsible and irredeemably different to whites prevailed. His father regarded the National Party as too soft on the race question and joined the ultra-right-wing Conservative Party, which still clung to the ideals of Hendrick Verwoerd. That his son chose to fly in the face of all of this and join the largest black organization in the country is evidence of the dramatic degree to which stereotypes are being challenged by the seismic changes in South Africa.

I was present at an ANC meeting in Cape Town where Nelson Mandela shared the platform with Wilhelm and his wife Melanie. There I heard a black and mixed race crowd chant 'Viva Verwoerd' and afterwards watched the people of the townships gather around their Afrikaner comrades.

It was obvious that there, in the milling crowds, the extended white hands of Wilhelm and Melanie Verwoerd were punching holes through the mist of suspicion which centuries of race supremacy had created. Nobody leaving that hall could ever again feel sure of the stereotypical image of Afrikaners as die-hard racists.

I admit that, when I first went to South Africa as a visiting journalist a decade ago, I arrived armed with a whole set of stereotypes. They essentially revolved around the notion of most whites being heartless and bigoted and most blacks being stoic and saintly. There was a good deal of truth in both stereotypes, but they failed to take account of the hidden strengths and weaknesses in human nature, and the essential fact of every human being's individuality.

Take, as an example, the jeweller with whom I had a furious argument in Cape Town, accusing him of being un-Christian and cruel because he did not fight against apartheid. I left his shop believing him to be a classic example of a callous white autocrat. He slotted neatly into my image of the white South African: fat, selfish and blind. I am sure that I, too, lived up to his stereotype of the young foreign visitor: naive, meddling and loud-mouthed.

We were both of us a little bit right, but experience has shown me the foolishness of viewing individuals through the prism of my own preconceptions. The jeweller was a far from attractive character, but I had not taken into account his personal fears and worries; what he was afraid of losing should the majority ever take over. Now, with the benefit of hindsight, I can attempt to see him as an individual, frightened and unsure with no means of escape.

Every day of life in South Africa produced encounters with people who seem to live up to one stereotype or another. Walk into a bar in any rural area and you will meet plenty of pot-bellied men with decidedly right-wing views. They are perfect fodder for visiting journalists because they can always be relied upon to deliver a racist quote and a blood-curdling warning of an apocalypse to come. But behind this racist haze there are surely people whose history and immediate circumstances are more complex than we, as journalists, often manage to convey.

A similar simplification takes place in the black townships. To outsiders, the youth seem anarchic and wild, straining at the leash to hurl themselves at the throat of white South Africa. These young people are frequently shown as petrol-bombing desperadoes and are described with depressing frequency as a 'lost generation'. Their white fellow-countrymen regard them with a great measure of apprehension, looking over their shoulders for the day when the hordes finally rise up and stream out of the townships into white suburbia.

And yet consider the thousands of children who attend the Chicken Farm school outside Johannesburg. Many of these children have grown up with war and poverty but still manage to don clean school uniform and travel several kilometres on foot to gain an education. There are many youths who are out of control but, again, the tendency to lump them together as a group or a generation is to deny their individuality. For each child who hurls a petrol bomb there is at least one more who is struggling to get to class and working for a better future.

In the future, black and white South Africans will live in a land where the constitution outlaws racism rather than actively encouraging it. This realization has already stimulated a huge process of readjustment, a slow coming to terms on the part of ordinary people caught up in the heave of history.

The racist stereotypes will not disappear overnight. Many whites will continue to regard blacks as sub-intelligent children who are unfit to rule; many blacks will look on whites as selfish and lacking in humanity. But those tempted to despair about the future of South Africa should remember that millions have already joined Wilhelm Verwoerd on the journey away from the apartheid past and its grand canvas of stereotypes.

THE INDISPENSABLE AFRIKANER

Johannesburg, January 1994

One of the questions being asked in the run-up to the multi-racial elections concerned the future status of the Afrikaner. Some had vowed to take up arms rather than be ruled by a black-dominated administration. But others had played a crucial role in the development of the South African economy.

Attie's fat sweating body barely squeezed into the khaki shorts and shirt of the Afrikaner Resistance Movement. Wads of flesh tumbled out over his waistband as he strutted up and down outside the hall where the 'great traitor' was speaking. Every few minutes Attie or one of the other right-wingers in the square would approach the police line and rail against the men in blue. How could they take the side of de Klerk and the blacks against their own people? Had they no self-respect left?

'You are Mandela's men,' a particularly vicious-looking youngster proclaimed, his right hand resting on the handle of a large automatic pistol. The policemen stood firm, refusing to be drawn into a verbal battle. Frustrated, Attie stormed away and sat down in the shade of a huge jacaranda tree. I approached tentatively and asked him why he hated de Klerk. At this the simmering frustration exploded. He stood up and answered in a great rush of beery breath. 'You people,' he declared, 'you think he's like Jesus Christ and you want the country to be destroyed by those black bastards. That's what you want.' Attie jabbed his finger hard into the centre of my chest and lowered his voice. 'Now listen, my friend,' he said, 'just take yourself and your communist pals out of here now. Move.'

Attie and his accomplices graced the screens of several television networks that evening, a menacing counterpoint to the pictures of the sweet reasonable President de Klerk. With their guns and fascist insignia and doom-laden prophecies of war, the legions of the extreme Right make excellent radio and television. Assuming he agrees to be interviewed, the average Boer extremist will readily testify to how blacks are mentally subnormal, how their wish is to drink and copulate all day, how they smell like sheep, and steal whenever the boss's back is turned.

The grand finale of any such interview is invariably a vow to fight to the death. This promise is frequently made with the subject posing in a field of maize, clutching a rifle and with several blond children, preferably armed, by his side. Thus, the rural Afrikaner is portrayed as the political and social Neanderthal, a creature far removed from the renaissance men who throng the ranks of de Klerk's reborn National Party.

These new Afrikaners wear smart suits and silk ties and are on chummy first-name terms with ANC leaders, and fall over themselves to announce that they had personally been against apartheid all along. With the pious faces of reverend mothers, they deliver chorus after chorus of self-justification and snicker up their sleeves at the country cousins. I have even heard a good many self-proclaimed liberals suggesting that what is needed is a short, sharp military clampdown to sort out the right-wingers once and for all. Once those rednecks are out of the way everything will be fine, they argue. There is more than a hint of malice abroad.

For the lazy journalist, this picture of neo-Nazi baboons on one side and the new moderates on the other provides a simple explanation of South Africa's current crisis. It is, of course, a gross distortion. The gun-toting fascists among the ranks of Afrikanerdom are comparatively few, in spite of the overwhelming prominence given them by journalists. Hidden by the simplifications of the mass media are the stoic majority who work hard and obey their God. They rise with the dawn and work until dark, they go to church on Sunday and are scrupulous about paying their debts, giving employment and housing to vast armies of black workers and their families.

Of course, they profited from apartheid. They ardently supported the mass evictions, the tribal homeland system and the ruthlessness of the security police. Without cheap black labour they would never have created the vast ranches of the heartland. But, in being guilty of the sin of profiting from apartheid, are they any different from the huge business conglomerates which built their empires on the backs of armies of black workers, while proclaiming themselves to be liberals? The rural Afrikaners were at least honest about their belief in white supremacy, refusing to cloak their language in the manner of the urban élite, which now rushes to condemn them.

In many ways they remind me of the dour Unionist farmers of County Antrim, possessed of a powerful sense of self-reliance and a flinty determination to hold fast to the land of their ancestors. Like the Ulster Protestants, they are outnumbered and live perpetually in fear of betrayal by politicians who hurry from one compromise to the next. The men who once urged them to worship apartheid are now scrambling to secure their places in the new power structure. The fact that F.W. de Klerk and most of his cabinet were, until a few years ago, ardent supporters of racial discrimination is conveniently forgotten in the rush to heap all the blame on the country bumpkins.

Even the Broederbond - Afrikanerdom's answer to the Masonic lodge - which controlled every level of government and engineered some of the worst cruelties of the apartheid years, has joined the ranks of the born-again multi-racialists. This organization, which sent police to scour people's beds for evidence of multi-racial sex, now speaks piously of the need to broaden the Afrikaner nation and include non-whites in its ranks. The sound of rodent battalions galloping from sinking ships is loud in the air. A new power élite is emerging, a conspiracy of political convenience from which the stolid farmers with their antique views are excluded.

That the rural Afrikaners are badly served by the leadership of the oafish Eugene Terre' Blanche and the politically naive General Constand Viljoen is undoubtedly true. The right-wing leaders have waited too long to define their objectives, and have now produced an unworkable plan for an ethnic white state. But to sweep the conservative Afrikaners aside as if they were archaic irrelevancies, or to suggest that they should be quelled by force of arms is dangerous nonsense. They would almost certainly lose a war, but the resultant economic chaos could easily reduce the country to a wasteland. Without them, South Africa would become a basket-case along the lines of Zaire or Zambia.

What is needed is less moral grandstanding on the part of the ANC/government alliance and its western friends, and more compassion and understanding. The people who turned the vast hinterland into thriving farmland should be treated as valued citizens, and not be subjected to the odium and rejection which has become their lot. Any half-sane country should fall over itself to nurture people like these, and not reduce them to the status of outlaws.

Take the example of Boet Van Rensburg, who farms several thousand acres on the rolling platteland about two hours drive east of Johannesburg. On the day I went to see him, teams of workers were busy in the fields tending the maize crop, others were hard at work in the dairy where a herd of fat Friesians was being lined up for milking. Everywhere there was movement and bustle. Boet strode out to greet me with a warm handshake and an offer of coffee.

As we passed through the sitting-room, I noticed a large

bible sitting on an ancient dresser. Above the dresser was a watercolour depicting a pastoral scene from the days of the Voortrekkers: a tiny white-washed cottage sat in the folds of a vast mountainscape, the trail of smoke rising from the chimney like a prayer in the emptiness of the land. Boet told me that the cottage was like the one his grandparents lived in before they trekked out of South Africa in the bitter years that followed the end of the Boer War. Defeated and disillusioned, they had crossed the Limpopo and travelled to Northern Rhodesia where they began farming deep in the bush. For a while they prospered in the adopted country, giving employment and producing food. Then came independence and the beginning of the country's slow economic death. The Van Rensburgs packed up and headed south to begin all over again on the platteland.

As he talked, Boet pointed to the photographs of dead relatives on the sitting-room walls. Most had died young of TB or malaria on farms which were hundreds of miles from the nearest hospital. Their thin grey faces spoke of hard lives and long journeys back and forth across the wilderness.

Boet wanted me to understand that he did not hate blacks. He did not call them kaffirs or beat them up, and he paid a living wage to his workers, as well as taking care of their food, housing and medical requirements. 'I just don't want to be ruled by them,' he said. He spoke of the rise in violent crime in the area, the break-ins and murders, and the endless theft of livestock and farm machinery. There was also the drought which ravaged the previous year's maize crop and turned the soil into dust.

All of this, he believed, could be linked to the political situation, as if the Afrikaners were being punished by God for relaxing their iron grip. 'Look what happened to us in Northern Rhodesia. They'll do the same here, just you watch. And then, when people are starving and the economy is in ruins, then they'll come to us for help,' said Boet. I asked whether he thought there would be a civil war of the kind predicted by Terre' Blanche and his stormtroopers. Boet flinched at the mention of his name. If people tried to take away his farm, then he would fight. But talking about war was a lot easier than actually going out and waging it. 'It is an easy way to lose everything,' he added. He clearly had as little time for the AWB as he had for the opposition.

Boet was determined to stay put. There would be no more trekking away to a new white homeland, no abandoning the land and the people who worked on it. All he wanted was the recognition that he and men like him could live in peace and security and not be treated as lepers. He was secretary of the local farmers' association and said his neighbours shared his feelings. They did not like what was happening but they recognized the reality of the situation. Unlike the Ulster Protestants, there was no large power willing to guarantee, however conditionally, their position: black rule was coming and it was a case of running to the city or making the best of things on the farm. Most were taking the second option. To abandon the land was a sacrilege that could not even be contemplated.

The sacred attachment to the land will, I believe, eventually save the rural Afrikaners from the folly of their leaders and the cynical manoeuvring of their opponents. The new regime might be tempted to treat them roughly, but the economic wasteland in the countries to the north should serve as a warning against alienating those who produce the food and create the wealth. Subtle changes in ANC attitudes towards the farmers suggest that South Africa's future leaders have realized this. A minority of right-wingers will probably take up arms and the situation will appear desperate for a while. But a mass uprising of Afrikaners seems distinctly improbable.

In their three-and-a-half centuries on the continent of

Africa, the Boers have watched the empires of the Dutch, the British, the Zulus and now their own fall away. Through it all they have maintained a simple belief in the certainty of their divine deliverance, a conviction which has enabled them to overcome the mightiest odds. It is that steadfastness which leads me to believe that men like Boet van Rensburg will be tilling the soil of Africa long after the pious braying of their critics has been swallowed up by history.

DOWN ON THE FARM

Piet Retief, February 1994

Life was becoming extremely difficult for black farm workers, a marginalized group at the best of times. They owned no land of their own and enjoyed few rights. The white farmers were becoming increasingly afraid of what might happen under black majority rule, and were starting to evict their staff.

The Swazi View Farm sits among the wooded hills that form South Africa's border with the independent kingdom of Swaziland. It is a farm devoted entirely to the breeding of vast armies of chickens for the dinner tables of the distant cities of the Witwatersrand. There are long blockhouses in which the doomed fowls pick relentlessly at grain, the noise of their clucking an endless soundtrack to life on the farm. Swazi View, like most farms in the area, is owned by an Afrikaans-speaking white man and is close to the town of Piet Retief named after a Voortrekker leader killed by the Zulus during the great trek of the last century.

Driving through this area one is struck by its pastoral beauty, by the blanket of calm which seems to cover the rolling farmland and the woods. There is a sense of timelessness, unique to the quiet spaces of the world, as if the noise of humankind had been swallowed up by the deep forests, its frantic pulse slowed in the presence of so much serenity.

But there is a darker, a much darker truth hidden by the glory of the landscape around Swazi View Farm and if one hears the story of Beki Hlope it's hard to ever again travel this way and hear only the uncomplicated silence of the trees.

Seventeen-year-old Beki was born and brought up on the farm, and lived with thirteen other members of his family in a two-roomed mud hut with one window. His uncle Philip Mlangeni was the supervisor on the farm and had been living there for decades. He earned around twenty pounds a month with rations in return for long days of hard work.

The farmer was a disciplinarian, according to Philip, and would refuse the monthly rations to all of the workers if one of them misbehaved. Neither was he a generous man, refusing to allow his workers the right to plant crops around their huts. This, Philip believes, was designed to maintain their dependence on him. But the real problems only began when Philip reported that some chickens had been stolen. A quarrel with the farmer ensued, and Philip was fired and his family told to leave the farm. It should be pointed out at this stage that the farmer regarded his supervisor as a troublemaker and frequently referred to him as Mandela.

The family held on as long as they could on the farm but, one night, about two weeks later, the farmer's son and two security guards arrived at the hut. Philip was away but his nephew Beki argued with the white boy. He then ran into the other room and was followed by the farmer's son and the guards. Beki's mother remembers the sound of her son begging for mercy and says he was beaten with a rifle. When the farmer's son and his accomplices left, Beki was lying on the floor making gurgling noises.

Now the family had no transport of their own and it took four hours to find someone who would drive them to hospital in Piet Retief. When they got there they were told Beki would have to be taken to Baragwanath Hospital more than four hours away in Soweto where more sophisticated treatment would be available. The boy was placed in the van and driven to Soweto where he died the following day. Not long after that the farmer succeeded in evicting the entire family. They were dispersed, some living wild among the trees, others seeking shelter with friends on neighbouring farms. But, even in their hour of desperation, they were faced with the task of having to bury the dead teenager. The alternative was for him to be given a pauper's burial in some vast cemetery in Soweto, far from where he had lived and died.

At this stage the South African Council of Churches intervened and persuaded the farmer to allow Beki to be buried at Swazi View. There were strict conditions attached: the funeral would begin at eight in the morning and have to be finished by midday. The farmer would watch over the ceremony with his gun, and workers on the farm were refused permission to attend. Some defied the ban and came anyway to hear preacher Busizwe Sibeko tell the farm-workers that their day would come. In a land of oppressed people, they were the most oppressed, he said.

The farmer did not hear this; he kept his distance, patrolling the perimeter of the little graveyard in his pickup truck, gun at the ready. At the grave Beki's mother and sister became hysterical, their shrieks and cries rising above the mourning of the other men and women who had known and loved the dead child. They left Swazi View in the afternoon, leaving behind a grave marked by a mound of stones. They placed the ragged clothes of the deceased on the grave. They were his only possessions. What hurts the family most now is that they will not be able to visit the grave again, unless the farmer undergoes a dramatic change of heart. Beki Hlope, a child of the new South Africa, will lie alone and unvisited.

THE LAND OF THE DEAD

1994

'There is a land of the living and a land of the dead, and the bridge is love, the only survival, the only meaning.'

Thornton Wilder, *The Bridge of San Luis Rey*

Although I could not have imagined or predicted it that night during my long drive back from the far Northern Transvaal, the ultra right wing was just weeks away from the act of self-destructive, arrogant stupidity that would drain the will of its support base and remove forever the threat of a widespread uprising against the incoming government. Yet for me, the events surrounding the first and last major military action by the right wing were to have devastating personal consequences, leading to the death of one of my closest friends and colleagues and propelling me into a long period of melancholy and questioning. They were to prove my darkest days in South Africa, days when my belief in the foreign correspondent's trade was severely tested and my worry over the future of the country at its most intense.

In those final rain-drenched days of February 1994, the far right represented much more of an unknown quantity than most journalists cared to admit. We would talk about the fascists endlessly, assessing their military capability, examining the mad maps for a white homeland as if there might be a grain of political possibility lurking somewhere between the arbitrary grid lines. Although we suspected them of being little more than overblown bullies who had little stomach for a fight, we could not be sure. Thus it became the accepted wisdom among the international press corps that, while most of the AWB's supporters were oafish loudmouths, there was a minority on the right that was well-armed and dedicated enough to seriously disrupt the election if it sought to do so.

There were endless rumours about former reconnaissance commandos of the South African Defence Force (SADF), an élite unit of the South African army that acted as a long-range scout and sabotage group during the bush war in Angola and Namibia, training groups of men in the mountains. It was even suggested that large groups of German and Croatian rightists had appeared in the country to put steel into the backbones of their South African counterparts.

Throughout the months of January, February and March speculation about the military intentions of the right wing increased. Although there were increasing signs that the pragmatists led by General Constand Viljoen wanted to ditch the AWB and take part in the election, the General continued to talk in two languages: one suggested joining the democratic process as a strategic alternative that would allow Afrikaners to argue the case for a white homeland from within; the other hinted at a joint course of political military action.

His press officer, a tense and obsessive young man named Stephen Manninger, had taken to carrying an automatic rifle and a pistol in public, and spoke alternately of the need for dialogue and of his willingness to fight against the 'Communist-dominated ANC'. Yet, like many of the thinking rightists, Manninger was beginning to understand what had long ago dawned on the leaders of the National Party: the demographic reality made it inevitable that black men and women would some day rule South Africa, all of South Africa. It was now a case of having to get the best deal possible within the parameters of that reality.

But even if most of us did ultimately believe in Viljoen's common sense and reluctance to go to war, the signals were vague enough to leave many journalists in a state of open confusion. The doubts were to be dispelled during a few insane days in the death of the Republic of Bophuthatswana.

The 'republic' consisted of six pieces of territory said to represent the traditional homeland of the Batswana tribe, South Africa's second-largest language group. These islands of land were scattered across the provinces of the Transvaal, the Orange Free State and the Cape, and surrounded by the white South Africa upon which Bophuthatswana was politically and financially dependent.

The fractured 'republic' had as its president one Lucas Manyane Mangope, a greedy and despotic tribal chief who crawled and stamped his way to the top with the help of South Africa's security establishment. For them, he represented the perfect puppet: a man who was quick to denounce racial discrimination but who was equally willing to praise the notion of 'separate development' as a means to achieve peace and prosperity.

Mangope was given a flag and a capital, Mmabatho, with its own parliamentary buildings and the great symbol of African pride, an Independence Stadium. Crucially, the President of Bophuthatswana was given his own security forces, with scores of South African advisers to help him crush any internal dissent.

In appearance Mangope looked like a man whose face was in the process of melting: the flesh sagged from his high cheekbones, while his lips seemed to curl outwards and down. His great dead eyes exuded contempt for the lesser beings who flitted in and out of his charmed circle. When he spoke it was with an unusually (for an African despot) soft and restrained voice, a voice that was both pompous and bored, which regarded the public explanation of his government's actions as an unnecessary and time-wasting exercise.

Lucas Mangope was born in 1923 into an old chiefly family in the north-western Transvaal, and on reaching the age of twenty-one he inherited the title of leader of the Mathlathowa clan of the Tswana tribe. Upon leaving school, Mangope studied as a trainee teacher and taught in schools throughout the north-west, an experience that should have given him ample insight into the wretched condition of black education.

Between the years 1952 and 1959, the formative years of apartheid, Mangope travelled from school to school and would have seen the steady destruction of black lives as the authorities moved to enforce the various acts that defined where the majority population could live, and what work it was entitled to do. But while the oppression of those years prompted many to join the liberation movements, propelling themselves towards death, jail or exile, Mangope opted for the inside track. He went back to his home region of Motswedi and inherited the chieftainship upon the death of his father in 1959. From then on it was a straightforward climb up the apartheid ladder from Chief of the Tribe to President of the Republic of Bophuthatswana.

The 'country' became formally independent in 1977 - the same year Steve Biko died in police custody - and Mangope's Bophuthatswana Democratic Party won every seat in the National Assembly. The vast majority of the population of this new republic refused to vote; having been stripped of their South African citizenship overnight, they were not about to endorse the move by voting for the fictive republic dreamed up by the apartheid master planners and their local puppet.

The President quickly made it clear that he would brook no serious internal opposition. Supporters of the ANC, members of the trade union movement and students all found themselves facing the guns of Mangope's thuggish security forces. For its part, the ANC set out to destabilize the Mangope regime using tactics of ungovernability that had caused so much trouble for Pretoria.

The campaign came to a head on the morning of 10

February 1988, when Mangope was confronted by soldiers and placed under arrest. Together with his senior cronies, the President was taken to the Independence Stadium to await a decision on his fate. It was a fatal misjudgement by the coup plotters. Within hours the SADF came streaming into Mmabatho, crushing the coup and freeing the President from his captors. There followed a purge of the armed forces and government departments with anyone suspected of disloyalty being summarily dismissed.

With the release of Mandela and the unbanning of the ANC in early 1990, Mangope's lease on power began to run out. Implicit in the whole process of negotiation was the principle that a united South Africa would emerge at the other end. Thus, while he took part in negotiations, Mangope could never have been in any doubt that the process signalled the end of his toy state.

As the ANC and the government reached deal after deal, Mangope moved into an alliance with the white right wing and Chief Buthelezi, arguing for an ethnic constellation of states and continually blustering about his determination not to be intimidated. He had as his chief negotiator one of Southern Africa's inveterate political carpet-baggers, the toupee-wearing Rowan Cronje, who had been a former member of the UDI (Unilateral Declaration of Independence) government of Ian Smith in Rhodesia and who had subsequently served in the administrations of Transkei and Ciskei, two of the other nominally independent states set up under apartheid.

Cronje presented a genial and reasonable face to the media and might well have signed up for the elections had he been able to persuade Mangope that there was more to be gained than lost from such a course of action. But Mangope deluded himself into believing that the alliance with Buthelezi and the far right and the power of his own security forces could hold the day.

Just months before the polling day Mangope opened an embassy in the Baltic republic of Latvia, to add to those he maintained in London and Washington. But of all the remaining members of the conservative Freedom Alliance he was the most vulnerable: his territory was scattered across South Africa, his patrons in Pretoria had deserted him and, unlike Buthelezi and General Viljoen, he had negligible political support.

Mangope bought the loyalty of his civil service and his security forces, but, when they began to realize that an ANC government was inevitable and that their pensions and jobs were in danger, they promptly turned on their benefactor. Thus it was in the final weeks of March 1994 that a wave of strikes, encouraged by the ANC, began to cripple the homeland administration and prepare the way for Mangope's downfall.

All morning the reports have been coming in and by now both myself and John Harrison are in a state of mounting anxiety. 'I knew we should have gone in yesterday,' says Harrison, who is pacing up and down the hallway. 'It'll take us at least three hours to drive to the bloody place and I'll never make it in time for the nine,' he adds before disappearing into his office.

I check the wires again and notice that the South African Press Association is now describing serious rioting in the centre of Mmabatho and its twin town of Mafeking. Upon hearing this, John jumps up from behind his desk and shouts out, 'There is nothing else for it - let's just hire a plane and get the bloody hell up there.'

In a matter of minutes this is organized and we are en route to Lanseria Airport. The BBC news television crew is already in Mmabatho and filming the disturbances. John had sent them ahead the previous day.

Once inside the cramped interior of our four-seater plane, John begins tapping his fingers on the case of his lap-top computer. 'I just hope to God we make it in time for the nine,' he says.

We climb through several layers of black cloud and the pilot warns that there is a storm coming from the north, the very direction in which we are heading. The plane begins to jump and bump, and I bang my head against the roof. John is giggling now, noticing the expressions of pure panic on the faces of myself and our two colleagues, Chris McGreal of the Guardian and Joan Leishmann of the Canadian Broadcasting Corporation. 'Don't worry, Keane, we'll be fine.' Heartened by this, I turn to him and say that I am never afraid in his company. 'As long as you're here we'll be fine,' I tell him. 'If you keep saying it, then it must be true,' he replies.

We have given John the nickname 'Basher' and suspect that he is secretly proud of it. It is a nickname bestowed because of his determination never to allow anybody or anything to stand in the way of his getting the story.

Soon the plane is circling above Mmabatho, and we are straining our eyes to see if there are any burning buildings or crowds on the streets. From where we are, all seems to be quiet. Inside the airport terminal, with its customs hall for Bophuthatswana's foreign visitors, there is no sign of activity. Mangope's police and customs officials appear to have abandoned their posts. The white manager of AVIS tells us not to worry but warns us to take care of the car. 'You won't be going near any townships, now, will you?' he asks. We lie and tell him all we want to do is drive around Mmabatho and Mafeking. John has already jumped into the car driven by his crew. They are Glenn Middleton, the cameraman, and Jerry Chabane, the sound recordist. Chabane is a native of Soweto, a quiet but tough operator who is Middleton's best friend. Together with John, they have covered some hair-raising scenes of violence in the past few months.

We drive in convoy into Mmabatho and then split up, the television crew going to the hotel to allow John to view their footage, and myself, McGreal and Leishmann heading into the town centre. There is debris all over the streets, upturned rubbish bins, huge rocks and acres of broken glass sparkling under the afternoon sun. Groups of youths are hanging around the street corners. A police van pulls up just in front of us and a sergeant jumps out. He grabs one of the youths and starts to beat him. But the others push forward and begin to remonstrate with the policeman. He listens to what they are saying, frees the youth and then retreats into the interior of the armoured car. We hear the sound of tear-gas being fired and suddenly a group of people comes surging around the corner pursued by another armoured vehicle. I notice little puffs of smoke coming from the window of the van. 'Fucking rubber bullets,' shouts McGreal from the back. We have all seen what these lumps of hard rubber can do to people's heads and so we make a beeline for the ANC offices.

At the door we are greeted by an extraordinary apparition: a woman in a mini-skirt and fishnet stockings wielding a huge shot-gun. She introduces herself as 'Comrade Sis' and welcomes us inside. The office is crammed with excited young men. They are speaking in Tswana, but the gestures and the English words scattered here and there − police, tear-gas − make it obvious that they are expecting an attack on the building.

Suddenly there is the sound of rocks bouncing against metal, followed by loud bangs and cheering and then the searing presence of tear-gas. A police van pulls up outside the door and a voice on a mega-phone begins calling on the occupants of the building to come outside. Comrade Sis fingers the shotgun nervously. 'Just let them come,' she says, assuring me that at close range the blast from her gun would stop several policemen in their tracks. She tells me there are several more guns in the building. The tear-gas is now beginning to choke us. We cannot see it, but our eyes are streaming and our lungs are beginning to heave.

The police eventually pull back from the building. Rioting in another part of the city has apparently relieved the siege of the ANC building. Outside on the streets the crowds have set up barricades of burning rubbish and tyres. Thick black smoke is rising into the sky, blending with the dusk, and the mood is changing. Whenever the police appear the crowds melt back into the side streets. No sooner have they disappeared than the road is thick with angry chanting youths.

Both McGreal and Leishmann are veterans of Central America's

wars and, like me, they have witnessed countless riots and civil disturbances. This, however, is different. There is a viciousness, a madness in
the air, that makes us all nervous. Anything can happen on these
streets. Bophuthatswana is in limbo-land — halfway between the
oppressive rule of Mangope and the clutch of the future. Nobody is sure
what the rules are, if there are any rules. We ask a police sergeant,
'Who is in charge here?' He pauses for a few seconds and then
answers, honest and confused. 'I don't know. Me, I really don't know.'

We drive to the township of Montshiwa outside the capital. There
are army checkpoints everywhere. They seem to have sprung up within
hours. On the road outside Mmabatho we meet a Reuters TV crew.
They are friends of mine from Johannesburg. Mark, a white South
African, and Frank, his black sound recordist, have been badly beaten
up. They are in a state of shock. Mark tells us how the army and police
dragged them out of the car and laid into them with batons and rifle
butts. Mark warns us to keep tape recorders and cameras well hidden.
'These guys are crazy, man — just keep your heads down,' Mark calls
out as we drive away. There are several checkpoints on the road to
Montshiwa, all of which we manage to negotiate safely. There are hos-
tile stares and endless questions, but we are left unmolested.

On the outskirts of the township our car is surrounded by several
hundred youngsters. I notice that many of them are carrying petrol
bombs and rocks. A large trench has been dug in the middle of the
road. The mob is very angry and we are being told to produce our ID
documents. We hand over ANC press cards and this mollifies the
crowd.

Behind us, Ken Oosterbroek, a photographer from the
Johannesburg Star, is being given the same treatment. Ken is a
cool customer and produces his ID and smiles his way through the
roadblock. Within six weeks Ken will be dead, shot dead in another
township, but on this morning he cannot see into the future, and he is
able to joke and laugh with us about the crazy situation.

When we get out of the car kids surge around us, shouting,
'Phantsi, Mangope, phantsi' (Away with Mangope, away). The

leader is a youth of about eighteen. 'Mangope, he must just go now. We never elected him and we don't want him. Tell him, you can tell him from us he must just go,' the unofficial spokesman says. One of them waves a petrol bomb in my face. 'You smell that. You like that,' he says before reeling back into the crowd, laughing aloud. It is time to leave.

Back at the hotel that evening I met John Harrison in the bar. He was excited, talking about the rumours that were circulating of a major march by students and civil servants the following day. But later I watched him having dinner with Glenn and Jerry and he seemed strangely quiet. There was none of his usual jocular banter. I put it down to him being tired. At forty-eight he acted and worked like a twenty-year-old, hauling himself from townships to press conferences to interviews without drawing a breath. Most of the time he seemed to blast his way through, without appearing to feel the effects of his punishing work schedule. Except occasionally he would crash, hiding himself in a dark room until the effects of the savage migraines he suffered went away.

John had covered more wars than anybody else in the South African press corps. He had been in Vietnam and Uganda, had covered the fall of Nixon and the rise of Thatcher. Having started his career on local newspapers, he became a domestic and later foreign correspondent on the *Daily Mail* and the *Daily Express* before moving to the BBC, where he rose to become Chief Political Correspondent. His blunt nature and fierce honesty made him an unsuitable candidate for the chumminess and double-talk common to the Palace of Westminster, and when the chance came to go back into the field in South Africa, he jumped.

Having spent much of his childhood on the move because of his father's job in the army, John knew what it was to have to prove himself again and again in new environments. In South Africa he seemed to have found the perfect niche. It was a place that gave plenty of scope to the determined individual, and John blossomed, completing project after project and always planning another.

Although he was a bright, curious man, he had an instinctive suspicion of intellectuals and was inclined to present the tougher side of his nature all too often. This was to the detriment of the sensitive and thoughtful part of his personality, which I had encountered in the quieter moments away from the job. Yet his no-nonsense attitude was something I and many others had reason to be thankful for on more than one occasion. In the heat of battle he could make you feel safe as no other individual I have known could manage. With John one felt secure. His presence was powerful, domineering, and seemed to cast a huge screen around those who travelled with him into the townships or to right-wing rallies. I had seen him dispatch young toughs in the townships with a clip around the ear, order spear-carrying warriors to stop intimidating journalists and, in one unforgettable moment, physically lift Eugene Terre' Blanche's bodyguard out of the way when he tried to prevent John from interviewing the neo-Nazi leader. He could be infuriating; driving his camera team as hard as he drove himself, arguing relentlessly, but his courage and generosity overcame any defects in his personality.

Like myself, John felt an intimate attachment to the South African story. It went beyond the ordinary interest of a journalist to the degree that the country's transition to democracy became a personal passion. He lived and breathed the story; for him it was a magical tale, a human drama in which he played the honourable role of participant/historian.

Unlike so many others in our profession, he did not regard the death and horror as vehicles for his own advancement. The massacres and the stupid waste horrified him, touching the core of his being. Because he was one of life's outsiders, perhaps because he had found himself on the receiving end of taunting and discrimination as a child, John identified with the suffering of the impoverished, the voteless and the abused.

He was at his best reporting from the marginal zone, from the edge where the lost and the broken hovered, their voices striving to be noticed. I knew from our many private conversations that he was looking forward to covering the elections as the biggest story of his career; for somebody who felt the story so intensely and who detested oppression as much as John did, the first non-racial election was an event to be savoured.

That night John went to bed early, stopping at my table to say goodnight and to make arrangements for coverage the following day. The next morning students from the University of Bophuthatswana began to arrive at the hotel, some of them talking excitedly about demonstrations that were being planned for that afternoon. John was among the first to head off in the direction of the university campus, a sprawling complex of hideous blockhouse buildings close to the city centre.

By the time I arrived, the rioting was in full swing. Clouds of black smoke were drifting across the campus from piles of burning rubbish, groups of students were roaming around armed with iron bars and rocks. The police made occasional sallies but retreated again under a hail of rocks.

A car pulled up and was immediately surrounded by the mob. A woman inside began to plead for her life. Someone in the crowd had recognized her as a government official. She began to cry hysterically. 'Out, out, out,' the mob shouted, shaking the car from side to side. A window was smashed and a youth reached in and began to beat the woman around the head. I threw caution to the wind and began screaming at them to stop. The crowd turned and some of the youths began to shove me backwards. 'Go away, man, this one is not your problem,' a student who was wearing a balaclava shouted into my face.

Suddenly the car bucked forward, surprising the crowd who jumped out of the way, giving the woman a few vital seconds to accelerate. She drove with the fear of one who could sense her life was seconds away from being extinguished. As the car sped on to the centre of the road, the crowd began to pound the vehicle with a barrage of rocks. I saw one of them crash through the passenger seat window and bounce off the woman's head. Blood spurted out and the car zig-zagged for a few moments. But her fear was greater than her pain and she managed to drive out of range, the car shuddering to a halt at a police roadblock further up the road. The police reacted with firing and began to advance down the road in armoured cars. Rubber bullets and tear-gas rained on to the campus. I jumped behind a wall, coughing and choking, but at least out of range of the police guns.

I kept looking for John, remembering our midday appointment and hoping that he had managed to get some footage of the riots. A photographer hiding behind the wall with me said he had seen John earlier, when the police launched their initial assault on the university. John had apparently filmed the action and then made a break to the nearby town of Zeerust to feed the story in time for the BBC's lunchtime news.

After spending several hours at the university, I decided to return to Johannesburg to collect some clothes and equipment. It was clearly going to be a long, difficult period and I was running out of clean laundry and tapes. Before checking out of the hotel, I tried to telephone John's room. The line was engaged and because I was in a hurry I decided not to walk up to the room and say goodbye.

It is late afternoon and I have left Mmabatho well behind. The weather is stifling hot and I roll down the car windows to feel the rush of air. It carries the hay-like scent of the mealie fields and I feel myself coming back to life. The land here is endlessly, relentlessly flat, pushing off into the distance for hundreds of kilometres, the tedium of the view broken only occasionally by the giant towers of grain silos and the even more occasional herd of cattle.

Somewhere south of Lichtenburg I notice a strange apparition in the distance. Because it is dusk, a time of a thousand shadows on the high veld, I am not sure if the distant convoy is what I think it is. Perhaps it is a line of delivery trucks on the way to Botswana or a huge pipe heading for one of the mines. But as the convoy comes closer, I notice that it is made up of SADF vehicles.

There are troop carriers with fifty millimetre cannons as well as smaller armoured cars with light machine-guns. The convoy comes alongside, I slow the car and shout to a black military policeman who is riding scout on a motorbike. 'Are you going to Bop?' I call out. He smiles and shouts back that they are going to sit on the border. 'We are on stand-by,' he says. At this stage I have to decide between going on or returning to Mmabatho straight away. I decide to keep going, reasoning that I am now so close to Johannesburg that it would make more sense to push on, collect my equipment and then race back.

By the time I get to Joburg it is dark and the radio news is talking about a fresh upsurge of rioting in Mmabatho. 'I can see people lying on the ground bleeding, this surgery is packed with the wounded,' a reporter on Radio 702 is saying.

As I walk into the office I can see my colleague, producer Peter Burdin, busy taking notes. He is white-faced and shaking his head. On seeing me, he looks up and mouths some words. 'John is dead,' I think he is saying. But he must be referring to somebody else. He puts the phone down and there are tears in his eyes. 'John is dead, mate — a car crash outside Mmabatho. I can't believe it, I just can't believe it,' he says.

I feel as if I have been kicked in the stomach. This is an idea I am not prepared to accept. It is as if my whole being rejects the notion that big, strong, loud, energetic John is dead. Peter is shaking as he tells me what he knows. There has been a bad accident outside Mmabatho. John and Glenn Middleton were rushing to the feedpoint. The car overturned as they went round a sharp bend. John died immediately. Glenn is in hospital but his injuries are not serious.

The voice at the other end of the phone talking to Peter belongs to a woman who witnessed the immediate aftermath of the crash. She heard a huge bang and ran out on to the road from her house. Although concussed and shocked Glenn had managed to give her the number of the office.

In a few minutes Glenn's wife Treacy arrives at the office. She is crying. A policeman has called her to say that John is dead and her husband is in hospital. 'What is happening?' she asks me, but I am unable to tell her. She gives me the name of the policeman and I call him. The facts are as the woman explained. John died immediately, his skull crushed when the car roof caved in.

At John's home the door is opened by his wife, Penny. She is one of the softest, kindest people I know. When she sees me and family friend François Marais, the expression on her face changes. I can see that she senses something and has been seized by fear. 'What is it? Something has happened to him, hasn't it?'

We do not know what to say, so we place our arms around her. 'Something very bad has happened. There's been a car crash,' I say. François picks up 'It was a very, very bad accident.' We go into the sitting room. 'Don't tell me, I don't want to hear you say it,' says Penny. 'I won't say it, Pen, I won't say it,' I reply.

And so we sit there, the room becoming emptier and emptier by the minute, the huge presence of John Harrison sucked out of the atmosphere. Friends of John and Penny begin to arrive in ones and twos. The telephone rings and a familiar voice asks for Penny. 'Please tell her it is Mr Mandela,' the man says. Later, President de Klerk's office rings. Soon every room in the house is full of people speaking in hushed voices; this is not real, this is a house suspended in a place of shadows.

The night seemed to last for ever. After calling the rest of the BBC staff together, I decided to drive back to Bophuthatswana in order to retrieve John's body and to bring Glenn Middleton back to a place of safety. The news reports coming out of

Mmabatho and Mafeking suggested a rapidly deteriorating situation; there were huge crowds on the streets, the police and army seemed to have split down the middle with rival factions exchanging fire. Nobody knew where Mangope was holding out. There were even rumours that he had fled to neighbouring Botswana.

What I knew for certain was that the body of my dead friend and an injured colleague were lying in the middle of a battle zone in a hospital that could be overrun at any moment. And so, in the early hours of the morning, I headed back to Mmabatho with my BBC colleague Milton Nkosi and two Canadian friends and journalists who volunteered to come along and help. It was a spectacularly starry night and we could see for miles across the veld, the lights of distant farmhouses blending into the canopy of the sky so that earth and heaven seemed to be one great portrait that spread before us.

We entered Mmabatho at around three a.m. and found the streets deserted, only a few soldiers milling around the main police station. The hospital was situated on the outskirts of Mafeking, the old Boer War siege town that lies directly adjacent to Mmabatho. It was a small building, more like a rural dispensary than a hospital catering to the needs of thousands of people. The main ward was filled with people who had been wounded in the previous day's fighting and a solitary nurse was making her rounds. She directed us to the room where Glenn was sleeping and told us we could take John's body away once the police had given the necessary clearance.

Glenn was bruised and severely concussed. We left him to sleep and went off in search of the police. At the main station a nervous guard cocked his weapon and advanced menacingly. Only the earnest pleading of Milton persuaded him that we were seeking their assistance and not planning to overrun the station.

Inside, several exhausted, red-eyed policemen sat slumped on the hard wooden benches of the large office. We explained our desire to remove the body and they listened patiently. 'You must come back in the morning. Can you not see we are over-stretched?' one of them asked.

The police force was at this stage struggling to make up its mind which side to join in the battle for Bophuthatswana. Some of the rank and file had already gone over to the ANC side, but the officers, like the men sitting in the charge office, were still loyal to Mangope. They had seen him survive the previous coup and were reluctant to put their careers, and possibly their lives, on the line to join an adventure that might yet be crushed. The memory of Mangope's purges of the security forces after the last uprising was fresh in the minds of the commanders, many of whom were promoted to fill the vacancies created by purged officers. The atmosphere inside the station was becoming tense and I sensed a growing impatience on the part of the man who had been answering our questions. We left offering profuse gratitude and promised to return in a few hours to talk to the day shift.

At the hotel, I slept for perhaps an hour and then woke up with a start, after dreaming that I could hear John's voice calling out above the sound of bullets and explosions. He had been shouting my name and telling me to follow him. It was the sound recording of some moment in the past suddenly hurled into my dreams, some fragment of a sentence uttered in a township long before when John was running hard and fast, blind to the future, to the death that was preparing to overtake him.

Now I was awake in the strange lost hours before the dawn, and could hear only the gentle sound of African birdsong on the patio outside my room. The light began to seep under the curtains, grey and uncertain at first, then flowering into the full bright glory of a late-summer morning.

Much of what happened later that morning has, thankfully, been lost to memory: I can remember a protracted debate with the police about the removal of the body; a steady stream of wounded arriving as the battle came closer and closer to the hospital; the road to the airport, our only exit, blocked by rioting mobs and finally by helicopters arriving to take us out. The first chopper was driven by a former airforce pilot. He had seen the mobs on the road as he circled above Mafeking. 'Shoot the whole fucking lot of them,' he said, 'that's what I would do. It's the only way, my friend. What is happening to this country?' Glenn and his wife Treacy, who had also arrived at the hospital, left on the first flight.

As soon as they had vanished into the sky, I went to the morgue to help lift John's body on to a stretcher. We could not find a body bag, so we wrapped him in blankets. How can I say what it felt like, this preparation for the journey home? Outside the mobs roamed the streets and soldiers were firing wildly, while here in a small concrete hut my friend slept an endless sleep, his energy and vigour now drained away. Now that I could see that mighty life-force reduced to stillness and silence, I was forced to accept that John Harrison was indeed dead. Dead. So hard to say the word, much less accept it.

There was no time for reflection just then, however. The sound of gunfire was louder and I could hear the cheering of the crowds coming closer. With the help of some hospital porters, we quickly loaded John's body on to the second helicopter. As the chopper lifted us up above the hospital, far above Mmabatho, I could see the smoke of burning barricades and the figures of the rioters like ant-people milling about in the streets below. And then we found ourselves over the veld, crossing the fields of green mealie plants and the farmhouses of the western Transvaal as the chopper flew east in the direction of Johannesburg.

There is something timeless about this journey. The chopper is a dream floating above the great flat spaces of the platteland. I am crammed in next to John; I can feel his arm wedged into my ribs, but I do not believe he is dead. We pass over herds of cattle and they run from the noise, the wap-wap of our rotors. Then we are crossing over an African village; there are mud huts with corrugated tin roofs and rusting cars lounging in the field alongside. Children rush out and wave at us; they are smiling and jumping, delighted by this great silver bird in the sky. I want to shake John and hear him laugh. He loved the innocence of children and these sweet angels in their ragged clothes are waving for him. 'Wake up, Johnny,' I say to myself. 'Can you hear them? Can you hear them?' But we sail on through the sky and behind us the children become specks on the horizon; they are like fragments of all the hope and possibility lost in the moment of John's death, and though they reach out to us, though they call his name on this late-summer wind, we cannot touch them or hear their sacred voices. We are lost.

By the time I had returned to Johannesburg with John, the situation in Bophuthatswana had deteriorated dramatically. The South African Army was reported to be preparing an invasion plan, but there were reports too of a mass gathering of right-wingers in Ventersdorp, the headquarters of the AWB.

There had also been a call on the right-wing Radio Pretoria for a general mobilization of Afrikaner Volksfront members. These were General Constand Viljoen's supporters, many of whom had gained their military experience during South Africa's bush war in Namibia and Angola in the seventies and eighties. Lucas Mangope, now hiding out on a farm in fear of his life, had called on the right wing to do the same job the South African Army had done several years before: save his government from the wrath of the people.

To the right wing, the call had a powerful resonance. Mangope was their kind of black, content to buy the idea of a Tswana nation state and an Afrikaner state on the simple basis that it guaranteed a life of wealth and power that a democratic settlement would never grant him. Though they would never say it openly, the President of the Republic represented the perfect Uncle Tom and if his republic were allowed to fall, the whole allied concept of a white nation state would be severely, if not permanently damaged.

That night, on farms across the platteland, men loaded supplies and ammunition onto pick-up trucks and set out for Ventersdorp. By early morning a convoy of some 400 right-wingers' vehicles was heading in the direction of Mmabatho, about two hours' drive from Venterdorp. This was to be the great adventure. The men in the convoy felt confident. They were armed to the teeth with shotguns, sniper rifles, automatic weapons and pistols. As far as they knew the Bophuthatswana security forces would support them. Their view of the potential opposition was shaped by the master-servant relationship on their farms. Well-fed and muscular, they could not imagine the scrawny boys of the Bophuthatswana townships being any match for them.

The right-wing army was a divided force, however. The Volksfront men tended to look down on the AWB, partly because of a genuine distaste for the neo-Nazi apparel and rhetoric, but also because many of Viljoen's supporters thought themselves socially a cut above Terre' Blanche's stormtroopers.

Viljoen attracted the big farmers and the intellectual right-wing; Terre' Blanche drew his strongest support from among the ranks of the poor whites and the smaller farmers who had most to lose from the economic and political upliftment of the black majority. To add to that was the very real contempt for Terre' Blanche felt by Viljoen himself and several of the other generals who made up the command council of the Volksfront. To them, the AWB leader was an oaf and a bully. Unlike Viljoen, he had never led men in combat, had never really known the reality of war. He drank too much and his much-publicized affair with the English-speaking columnist, Jani Allan, was just the kind of business to mortify the stolid Calvinist souls of the generals. In short, they regarded him as a fool, albeit a dangerous one.

The cracks in the right-wing alliance were to be glaringly exposed later in the day. But, for the time being, a semblance of togetherness was maintained. On arriving in Mmabatho, the right-wingers headed straight away for the airforce base, where Mangope had arranged for them to rendezvous with some of his senior officers. As the dawn came up, the main runway was witness to the extraordinary spectacle of right-wingers marching and drilling while others roared around in pick-ups. They began to patrol Mmabatho and Mafeking.

All this time, the South African Army stood on the border, awaiting instructions from Pretoria. Almost everybody in Bophuthatswana knew that, once the SADF did move in, the trouble would end. It had a reputation as a no-nonsense force and easily out-gunned the right-wingers, the Bophuthatswana security forces and the ANC's young militants.

The explanation advanced for the delay by political and military sources in Pretoria was that Bophuthatswana was still a constitutionally independent state (in terms of South Africa's constitution, that is) and a military invasion could take place only if Mangope requested it, or if his government ceased to function and exist. There were others within the military establishment who suggested to me that the decision to wait may have been prompted by a desire to see the right wing humiliated on the streets of Mmabatho and Mafeking. Whatever the reason, the delay helped contribute to the bloodshed and chaos that were to engulf the two towns later that morning.

The trouble began when sections of the Bophuthatswana Army refused to co-operate with the right-wing army. Weapons that had been promised to the white army were refused and racial insults were exchanged between rival groups at the airforce base. Finally, under pressure of invasion from Pretoria, Mangope was forced to issue a statement calling on the right-wingers to withdraw from Bophuthatswana.

As the news was filtering through, a blazing row erupted between leaders of the AWB and Volksfront contingents. Jannie Breytenbach, brother of the poet Breyten and a former special forces commander, publicly denounced the AWB and accused them of being unfit for military duty. Amid a welter of bitter abuse and angry gestures, some of the right-wingers began to trickle out of Mmabatho.

As they left, one group of AWB members encountered an ANC crowd that was dancing at the side of the street. Someone in the AWB opened fire. Within a few seconds, units of the Bophuthatswana Army that had been following the AWB attacked the right-wingers. One car was hit while the others sped away.

After a brief fire-fight, the occupants of the car, all of them wearing the camouflaged uniforms and swastika-like insignia of the AWB, rolled out on to the ground. One was dead, the two others wounded. The survivors lay in the dust, pleading with journalists to get an ambulance. They said they had come because Viljoen had given an order for general mobilization. For more than half an hour they lay there being photographed and filmed by a large contingent of journalists. No ambulance came. 'For fuck's sake, will you please get an ambulance,' one of them pleaded. It was strange beyond words for black soldiers to see uniformed white men lying on the ground like this, begging for help.

A friend of mine who witnessed the incident told me he was afraid to go for assistance. The soldiers were angry and he was convinced they would have killed him had he moved. Then suddenly a soldier walked up to the AWB men and shot them dead at point-blank range. He screamed as he opened fire. It was a terrible moment and yet inevitable. The belief that blacks would melt away in the face of white firepower, that a white South African somehow carried an aura of untouchability when he confronted a black in battle, was punctured for ever.

Right-wingers who had heard about the execution went storming out of town, shooting at black civilians as they went. Three were gunned down in cold blood within hours. White journalists who approached the right-wingers were badly beaten up.

The departure of most of the right-wing contingent sparked off a major bout of looting in the centre of Mmabatho. A huge shopping complex known as MegaCity, reputedly owned by Mangope's cabinet ministers, was picked clean. I watched thousands of people swarm out of the building carrying suites of furniture, whole sides of beef, washing machines, everything that could be carried. A lone soldier fired a few shots in the air, but the Bophuthatswana Army had clearly given up any hope of stopping the looting.

After I had been there about an hour a rumour began to sweep through the crowd. The South African Army was on the outskirts of the town. They were coming this way. People began to flee, some of them dropping their valuables as they raced across the carpark in front of MegaCity.

I was driving back across the city, in search of the South Africans, when a group of armed men jumped into the road and began levelling their rifles and motioning for me to stop. I put my head down and accelerated through. In retrospect it was a foolish thing to do, but I was frightened and tired and felt certain they wanted to kill me. The combination of fear and deep anger over John's death had filled me with a kind of desperation. I wanted to get this story over and done with, to get the hell out of Bophuthatswana as quickly as I could. Luckily, they did not shoot and I made it through to see the first South

African columns rolling into Mmabatho. Groups of locals waved and cheered as the armoured vehicles drove into town.

That night, I watched them escort the remaining right-wingers out of town. The men who had entered Mmabatho swaggering and boasting now crept out of town under the protecting guns of the South African Army. It would be hard to conceive the depth of humiliation felt in right-wing circles as a result of the debacle in Bophuthatswana.

The following day General Constand Viljoen called a news conference in Pretoria and announced that he would henceforth refuse to take part in military actions involving the AWB. It was only a short step to a final split and a further announcement a week later from Viljoen that he would participate in the elections. Terre' Blanche was left isolated and humiliated. His boast that he would 'level the ANC with the grave' was shown up for the hollow flourish of rhetoric it really was.

Mangope was removed from power and two administrators, one black and one white, were installed in his place. The make-believe country set up to prove that apartheid could work had disappeared. There was jubilation on the part of the ANC, which had worked so hard to engineer Mangope's downfall. The President himself retreated to one of his many farms, muttering about court actions. Unusually for an African dictator ousted by popular revolt, he was neither killed nor imprisoned. He was left to a sullen silence and the enjoyment of the vast wealth he had appropriated during his years as supreme ruler of the supreme bantustan.

The overthrow of Mangope by a combination of people power and South African intervention was to have a profound impact not only on the right wing, splitting it irrevocably, but also on the politics of Natal, the country's bloodiest battleground. The collapse of the homeland regime was watched nervously from Ulundi, capital of Chief Buthelezi's KwaZulu homeland, where rumblings of secession and rebellion had been growing since Inkatha's refusal to sign the interim constitution the previous November. It was there that the next great acts in the death of the apartheid state were to be played out.

Bophuthatswana has fallen. Mangope is a bad joke from the past and everyone is shifting their focus to Buthelezi. But John Harrison is still dead. It is a week since the battle of Mmabatho, and we have gathered in Johannesburg to bury our colleague. It is a hot day of brilliant sunshine and mourners arrive in small groups at a small Anglican church in the northern suburbs. As we sit in the church, blissfully cool after the heat outside, they begin to play a tape of his favourite songs. I listen to Jagger sing 'Hey you, get off my cloud,' and I can see John elbowing his way to the front of the crowd at a news conference or shoving some heavy out of the way as he creates space for Glenn to film.

In front of us, John's wife, Penny, sits flanked by their sons, Paul and James. Behind us, is Glenn Middleton staring straight ahead, his gaze focused on a stained-glass window behind the altar. There are prayers and words of praise for John. The minister talks about the tragedy of John never seeing a democratic South Africa. He asks everybody to pray for peace. The cleaners from the BBC offices stand up and begin to sing in sweet, mournful voices, 'Senzenina, senzenina,' ('God, what have we done to deserve this?'). Although I have heard this hymn at countless funerals, today for the first time it reaches deep inside me.

It is with difficulty, struggling to find a steady voice, that I go to the pulpit and talk about the life-force that has been taken away. 'He was not a human being, he was a force of nature,' I say. But what can anyone add to ease the pain of this most final goodbye. He was doing the job he loved, but there was so much more he wanted to do.

Yes, it is surely a glorious thing to witness the birth of democracy in South Africa. But I cannot at this moment, looking at John's coffin, at his grieving widow and sons, have any belief in the world I have chosen to live and work in. And, although I am ashamed to admit it, I have begun to fear for my own life. I look at the coffin of my friend and feel afraid for myself, as if the thousand risks we had taken together were adding up and my turn would come soon: perhaps in some wretched township; or at the hands of the neo-Nazis or in the hills of Natal; or maybe like John it would be a death of chance on a road somewhere. There would be tributes from my managers and colleagues, my wife and family would be heartbroken, but South Africa and all the other news stories in the world would go on, with men and women risking their lives to report them. And would a single reporter's death be worth it? Damn sure it wouldn't.

Filing out of the church into the sunlight, we listen to the flautist playing 'Amazing Grace'. But I feel nothing like grace. In fact I am gripped with hatred for the country. Although this is not noble to admit, I am sick of its insane and savage violence and the nightmares it gives me. As for the holy trade of the foreign correspondent, I have begun to doubt everything we represent. I am possessed by the feeling that the reporting of South Africa has become a commodity, a three-minute simplification of 300 years of history wrapped up in well-worn phrases. Journalists race around in search of civil war, secretly happiest when they sign off from some hell-hole where the bodies are stacking up and the omens of apocalypse are most vivid. I am sick to the teeth of war stories, the flak jackets and all the attendant bullshit. Why did we all do it? Why do people like John and me and countless others race around townships and battle zones? I am still searching for the answer, but I know that pursuit of the truth is only one part of the equation.

In the evening, we are standing in John's garden, surounded by a host of memories. The sky is low and overcast and the rain will come soon. People are drifting around with glasses of wine, seeking comfort from one another. I want to cry but no tears come. I want to cry for John and all the dead of the past three years but the emotion stays bottled up inside. I am lost and angry and confused and John Harrison is dead and gone for ever.

One last memory three weeks before John's death and we are in

Natal on the way to a funeral. A group of teenagers have been murdered while campaigning for the ANC. As usual, John has gone ahead
to get some shots at dusk. I am on the road with Milton Nkosi when
we see a car stopped in the middle of the road, its hazard lights flashing and headlights beaming straight ahead. 'Don't fucking stop, don't
stop, it could be a fucking ambush, just keep going,' shouts Milton. I
accelerate but notice as we approach, that the car is John Harrison's.
He is standing in the roadway — Glenn Middleton and Jerry Chabane
are there too. Just in front of the car is the body of a black man. He is
naked from the waist upwards and his body is covered in blood.

I stop the car and talk to John. He tells me they came across the
body in the road a few minutes beforehand. The man had been badly
beaten and was dead, but the few cars that were on the road would not
dream of stopping. Only John did. 'You can't leave the poor bastard
lying there like that, can you?' he asks. He gets a blanket from the boot
of his car and places it over the dead man. A few minutes later, a police
van comes along on a routine patrol and they remove the body.
'Sometimes this fucking country ...' John says, but I lose the end of the
sentence as he walks away into the dark towards his car.

POEM FOR JOHN

May 1994

Dead. So hard to say that word, to believe it.
So I will choose not to. Rather I imagine that
any moment now you will come rolling in the door,
a ship of life, bound for the shores of promise.

Dear, lost friend, we will harbour your memory,
we will bind our loss in the warm currents of
your laughter; we will search the African sky
for your wild, blazing star.

In the long term, the picture will become less
clear, we will all of us drift into other lives;
but your voice will endure, singing out to us
between the spaces in the wind, always free,
always John.

SEASON OF BLOOD

Nyarubuye, Rwanda, 1994

Up to a million people lost their lives when the shooting down of
President Habyarimana's jet led to a hundred-day orgy of killing
in Rwanda.

This was always going to be the hardest part, this remembrance of
what lay ahead in the dusk on that night in early June. My dreams are
the fruit of this journey down the dirt road to Nyarubuye. How do I
write this, how do I do justice to what awaits at the end of this road?
As simply as possible. This is not a subject for fine words.

We bounce and jolt along the rutted track on an evening of soft,
golden light. The air is sweet with the smell of warm savannah grass.
Clouds of midges hover around the cars, dancing through the windows. Although I can sense the nervousness of everybody in the car, we
are exhausted and hungry from the long day's travelling, and we are
too tired to bother fighting off the insects. Moses, our driver, shifts
down into first gear as we face into a long climb. The wheels begin to
lose their grip and they spin in the loose sand of the incline. 'Oh, shit,'
mutters Moses. We climb out and begin to shove and push, but the car
rolls back down the hill and we have to jump out of the way.

From the top of the hill we can see a great expanse of yellow
savannah grass, dotted here and there with thornbush and acacia.
Glenn, the cameraman, says it reminds him of home. He is right. This
could be the bushveld around Louis Trichardt in the far Northern
Transvaal.

After about fifteen minutes of manoeuvring, Moses eventually
gets the car going again and we move off. Frank, the Rwandan
Patriotic Front (RPF) soldier who is acting as our guide, has become
very quiet and he is fingering the stock of his assault rifle. After about
another fifteen minutes we come to a straight stretch of track, wider

than before and with a line of tall trees on either side. Up ahead is the façade of a church built from red sandstone. 'This is Nyarubuye,' says Frank. Moses begins to slow the car down and Glenn is preparing his camera to film.

As we drive closer, the front porch of the church comes into view. There is a white marble statue of Christ above the door with hands outstretched. Below it is a banner proclaiming the celebration of Easter, and below that there is the body of a man lying across the steps, his knees buckled underneath his body and his arms cast behind his head. Moses stops the car but he stays hunched over the wheel and I notice that he is looking down at his feet.

I get out and start to follow Frank across the open ground in front of the church. Weeds and summer grasses have begun to cover the gravel. Immediately in front of us is a set of classrooms and next to that a gateway leading into the garden of the church complex. As I walk towards the gate, I must make a detour to avoid the bodies of several people. There is a child who has been decapitated and there are three other corpses splayed on the ground.

Closer to the gate Frank lifts a handkerchief to his nose because there is a smell unlike anything I have ever experienced. I stop for a moment and pull out my own piece of cloth, pressing it to my face. Inside the gate the trail continues. The dead lie on either side of the pathway. A woman on her side, an expression of surprise on her face, her mouth open and a deep gash in her head. She is wearing a red cardigan and a blue dress but the clothes have begun to rot away, revealing the decaying body underneath.

I must walk on, stepping over the corpse of a tall man who lies directly across the path, and feeling the grass brush against my legs, I look down to my left and see a child who has been hacked almost into two pieces. The body is in a state of advanced decay and I cannot tell if it is a girl or a boy. I begin to pray myself. 'Our Father who art in heaven ...' These are prayers I have not said since my childhood but I need them now.

We come to an area of wildly overgrown vegetation where there are many flies in the air. The smell is unbearable here. I feel my stomach heave and my throat is completely dry. And then in front of me I see a group of corpses. They are young and old, men and women, and they are gathered in front of the door of the church offices. How many are there? I think perhaps a hundred, but it is hard to tell. The bodies seem to be melting away. Such terrible faces. Horror, fear, pain, abandonment. I cannot think of prayers now. Here the dead have no dignity. They are twisted and turned into grotesque shapes, and the rains have left pools of stagnant, stinking water all around them.

They must have fled here in a group, crowded in next to the doorway, an easy target for the machetes and the grenades. I look around at my colleagues and there are tears in the eyes of our sound recordist, Tony. Glenn is filming, but he stops every few seconds to cough. Frank and Valence, our other guide, have wandered away from us into a clump of trees and the older man is explaining something to the boy. I do not know what he is saying, but Valence is looking at him intensely. I stay close to our team leader David Harrison, a BBC producer with long experience of Africa, because at this moment, I need his age and strength and wisdom. He is very calm, whispering into Glenn's ear from time to time with suggestions, and moving quietly. The dead are everywhere.

We pass a classroom and inside a mother is lying in the corner surrounded by four children. The chalk marks from the last lesson in mathematics are still on the board. But the desks have been upturned by the killers. It looks as if the woman and her children had tried to hide underneath the desks. We pass around the corner and I step over the remains of a small boy. Again he has been decapitated. To my immediate left is a large room filled with bodies. There is blood, rust-coloured now with the passing weeks, smeared on the walls. I do not know what else to say about the bodies because I have already seen so much.

As we pass back across the open ground in front of the church I notice Moses and his fellow-driver Edward standing by the cars and I motion to them to switch on the headlights because it is growing dark. The sound of insects grows louder now, filling in the churchyard silence. David and the crew have gone into the church and I follow them inside, passing a pile of bones and rags. There are other bodies between the pews and another pile of bones at the foot of the statue of the Virgin Mary. In a cloister, next to the holy water fountain, a man lies with his arms over his head. He must have died shielding himself from the machete blows.

'This is fucking unbelievable,' whispers Tony into my ear. We are all whispering, as if somehow we might wake the dead with our voices. 'It is just fucking unbelievable. Can you imagine what these poor bastards went through?' he continues. And I answer that no, I cannot imagine it because my powers of visualization cannot possibly encompass the magnitude of the terror. David and Glenn say nothing at all and Frank has also lapsed into silence. Valence has gone to join the drivers. I do not know the things Valence has seen before this and he will not talk about them. I imagine that the sight of these bodies is bringing back unwelcome memories.

Outside the church the night has come down thick and heavy. Tony shines a camera light to guide our way. Even with this and the car lights I nearly trip on the corpse of a woman that is lying in the grass. Moths are dancing around the lights as I reach the sanctuary of the car.

While we are waiting for Glenn and Tony to pack the equipment away, we hear a noise coming from one of the rooms of the dead. I turn to Moses and Edward. 'What is that? Did you hear that?' I ask. Edward notices the edge of fear in my voice and strains his ear to listen. But there is no more sound. 'It is only rats, only rats,' says Moses. As we turn to go we look back and in the darkness see the form of the marble Christ gazing down on the dead. The rats scuttle in the classrooms again.

There was little talk on the way back to the main road. Tony produced one of our whisky bottles and we passed it around. I took several long draughts and lit a cigarette and noticed then that my hands were shaking. Frank watched the road ahead closely and told Moses to drive as quickly as he could. The men who had done the killing, the Interahamwe of Rusomo Commune and Nyarubuye itself, might have fled to Tanzania, but they crossed the border at night to stage guerrilla attacks and to kill any Tutsis who might have escaped the massacres.

I should have felt fear at that moment, but I had too much anger inside. After a long silence it was Moses who spoke. 'How can they do that to people, to children? Just how can they do it?' he asked. Nobody answered him and he said nothing else.

The journey back to the main road seemed to last an eternity. All along the way I could think only of the churchyard and the dead lying there in the dark.

Although the sight of the massacre made me feel ill, I was not frightened of the dead. They were not the source of evil that filled the air at Nyarubuye and that now began to undermine my belief in life. Now that we had left, the killing ground would be quiet again. Perhaps the militiamen passed there from time to time as they crossed back and forth into Tanzania. Were they still able to pass the scene of their crimes without feeling guilt? Did the rotting dead frighten them? The killers must have moved in close to their victims. Close enough to touch their shaking bodies and smell their fear. Were there faces among the crowd that they recognized? After all, the militiamen came from the same neighbourhood. Some of them must have been on speaking terms with the people who pleaded for mercy.

I thought of Seamus Heaney's line about 'Each neighbourly murder' in the backroads of County Fermanagh. Back in the north of Ireland I had reported on numerous cases of people being murdered by men who worked with them or who bought cattle and land from them. In Rwanda that intimate slaughter was multiplied by tens of thousands.

By the time we reached the main road again it was nearly

midnight. We have been warned sternly against travelling late at night on Rwanda's roads, even inside areas that were controlled by rebel forces. The militia were one problem, nervous sentries sitting in some lonely outpost were another, a potentially more dangerous one. Frank warned Moses to approach each check-point slowly with headlights dipped. He needn't have worried. Moses, veteran of Amin's Uganda, knew his way around mili-tary checkpoints and was punctiliously slow and precise when he pulled up to the blockades. The soldiers were less friendly at night. Even Frank with all his ease of manner could not punc-ture the atmosphere of sullen fear at the dark roadblocks.

We had passed the last roadblock before Rusomo Commune when the headlights picked out the figures of six or more people struggling wearily along the road. I called out to Moses to stop just ahead of them.

As we pulled in to the roadside I noticed that the group, a woman, three men and two small children, had halted in their tracks. They stood looking from our car back to the Land Rover carrying Glenn and Tony. The men were tall and thin and car-ried bows and arrows. One clutched a large rooster under his arm. The creature's legs had been fastened together and its beak tied up. The woman held a baby in the cradle of her left arm and, as I approached, I saw that the child was sucking relentlessly at one of her withered breasts. The woman was covered in dust and her face was gaunt. She would not look directly at us, but kept a stare fixed on the ground. Clinging to her legs was a small boy of around six.

'Who are you?' asked Frank. The woman began to speak but her words came in a soft foggy voice. We could only hear isolated snatches of the sentence. Frank came closer and spoke again. 'It is all right, my dear, we are not here to harm you. Please speak louder and tell us who you are.' She spoke again, this time in a voice that was still difficult to hear, but Frank, standing close by, was able to translate.

The woman had come from the area of Nyarubuye with the two small children. They had been hiding in the fields for more than a month when the three men had found them. At first she had feared that the men were militia and that she and the children would be killed. But one of the men, the one named Silas, was a neighbour and she knew him to be a Tutsi like herself. 'How did you survive?' asked Frank. 'We hid in the places of wild countryside and covered ourselves with grass and bushes and we ate roots and berries. We were eating grass like the cows. There were bodies everywhere dumped in the fields and ditches. It was hard and I thought we would starve to death. This would have happened if the men had not found us,' she replied.

For four long weeks this woman and children had watched from their hiding place as the killers scoured the countryside around them. Not once did the baby or the small boy cry out. She did not know why this was except perhaps that the children must have had some inner sense of the danger. Throughout the conversation the small boy twisted and turned around the woman's legs.

The man named Silas spoke up and said that the boy was not her child. His parents had been killed at Nyarubuye and he had escaped into the countryside. Somehow he had met up with the woman and her baby, and together the small group had evaded the militia bands who were hunting down survivors. The woman was alive because she had not gone to Nyarubuye with the other Tutsis. They had mistakenly believed that they would find sanctuary in the house of God. Some instinct had told her that the church was the least safe place to be. The woman's husband was gone, however. She would only say the word 'Gone' as if unable to admit that he had joined the ranks of the dead.

Although the woman seemed weary beyond words, the group was heading deeper into rebel-held territory, as far away from the border and the predatory bands of Interahamwe as they could go. Having survived once, she was not about to gamble with her life and those of the children. They said good-bye and began to walk slowly down the road. The little boy glanced backwards occasionally until we could see them no more.

That night we arrive at the Office of the Bourgmestre of Rusomo, Sylvestre Gacumbitsi. He has fled to Tanzania along with the Hutu population of the area. The building has several offices and also houses a health centre. There are piles of syringes and boxes of condoms. On the floor in the main office is the Rwandan flag, the flag of the old regime. It is green, yellow and red with a large black 'R' in the middle. Somebody has laid it across the floor so that it looks like a brightly coloured doormat.

The building has sustained almost no war damage, and the rebels have not looted the stores of medical and office equipment. Most poignantly, in a room at the very back is a library of index cards. These are in fact the identity cards of every local resident. There are thousands of these thin paper cards on to which are fixed the photographs of the bearers. Each card is marked with the name, address and ethnic identity of the resident, Hutu, Tutsi, Twa or other. Dust has gathered on the cards, and when I flick through it rises up and stings my eyes and nose. The colonial government introduced this system of population registration and their Rwandan Hutu successors entrenched it as a means of political control.

I have seen cards like these before, back in the bad old apartheid days in South Africa. They used to call them passbooks — little books that dictated who you were and where you could live. These cards are similar but I know that they have been used as instruments of geno-cide. With the ethnic identity and address of every resident registered here at the commune building, the Interahamwe had a ready-made death list.

I look at face after face of Tutsis and wonder if any are still alive.

Anybody who imagines that the killing was an arbitrary and disorganized tribal bloodbath had better come here. I have no doubt that this is an index list for murder, prepared years in advance and held in readiness for the day when the Tutsis might need to be sorted out.

In a room at the front, there are two RPF women soldiers patiently typing out passes for refugees. Many have fled here from far away and want to get home. The RPF has set up a reception centre for Tutsi refugees, where there is at least physical security and some small amount of medical care.

As we prepare to bed down in one of the old offices, Frank comes in and motions to David and myself to follow him. 'There are some survivors here, some survivors of Nyarubuye.' His voice is unusually excited and we follow him to a small room from where the light of a candle flickers against the glass panes of the doorway. The room is tiny, perhaps big enough for two people. There are six patients lying on mattresses inside. There is a smell of disinfectant mixed with the bad smell of septic wounds.

Of the six patients, five are children. One little girl lies in the corner, her head and hands heavily bandaged. A nurse comes in to change her dressings and she cries out, not loudly, but with a soft whimpering sound. David kneels down and begins to comfort her. As the nurse peels off the bandage on her head the girl grits her teeth. Underneath is a deep, black gash. The wound is festering. Some adult hit this child on the head with a machete and when she raised her hands to ward off the blows he struck her fingers because they too are mutilated and black. Her name is Varentina and she is not expected to survive the gangrene that has infected the wounds.

There are no painkillers here. Anything that might have been of use to the rebels was taken into Tanzania by the escaping Hutus. I go outside and fetch Tony, who is our medic on the journey. He brings Panadol, pitifully inadequate to stem the terrible pain, but it is all we have. The small white tablets are given to the nurse, who shares them out among the wounded.

The older woman is complaining of a terrible pain in her head.

She rocks back and forth, crying. The nurse pulls back her shawl and reveals a terrible deep wound to the skull. The woman rubs her hand against the wound and continues to cry. The other children are used to this because they pay more attention to us than to anything else that is taking place.

David goes outside and comes back several minutes later with a bag full of sweets. He had bought these back from Kampala and in his fatherly way doled them out to us as lunch on our journey down from the border. Methodically and gently, he goes from child to child and hands out sweets. They do not grab the sweets but quietly place them in their mouths.

The woman holds out her hand, thanks us, turns to the children and reminds them to say thank you. She tells us that her name is Flora Mukampore, a Tutsi from the area of Nyarubuye. 'Come in the morning,' she says, 'come in the morning and I will tell you the story of what happened to us there.'

They had heard, Flora Mukampore said, the news about the plane crash, in which the presidents of Rwanda and Burundi had died, from some Tutsi neighbours who had heard the story on the radio. Everybody knew it would be bad. The militias had been training in the area for a long time, months and months. The Tutsis knew about lists of people that were going around, lists of Tutsis to be killed. These names were being circulated among the Interahamwe and the police for weeks ahead of the plane crash.

The killing started soon after the crash on 6 April. Gangs of militia were going through the hills with whistles. They blew on the whistles to make the Tutsis come out of their homes. Many of these men were drunk and they had a look of madness in their eyes. They set fire to the huts of the Tutsis and took their cattle. It was death for any Tutsi who was in their way. The closer the gangs got to Nyarubuye the more frightened the Tutsis became. Some of their Hutu neighbours were kind and offered to help them. But they were threatened by others who promised to tell the Interahamwe. It was worst at night. There was screaming and shooting and people were waiting to die.

The Tutsis decided to form a deputation and went to Rusomo to see the Bourgmestre, Sylvestre Gacumbitsi. He was a big man in the area, a member of President Habyarimana's political party, the MRND, and he had power with the police and army. Without his help, the Tutsis knew that it was only a matter of time before they were all killed. Some of the Tutsis did business with Gacumbitsi. Somebody said his personal driver was a Tutsi. They believed that only the Bourgmestre could save them now. But when they went to see him, he turned them away.

Gacumbitsi would not give them protection. He told them to go to the church and try to find safety there. The people were shocked by this and they believed they would definitely be killed unless they defended themselves. The word spread quickly and thousands of Tutsis from the surrounding area fled to the church at Nyarubuye. People came with their children and their livestock and whatever they could carry. Flora Mukampore had gone with her husband's family. The priests and the sisters were kind but more and more people kept coming and there was very little space. The men had bows and arrows and spears. Some of the boys gathered as many stones as they could. People set up camp and waited. Many went into the church and prayed for deliverance.

It was not long before the militia arrived at the church and began to attack the refugees. People screamed and there was panic among the children. But the men and boys were able to drive them away with their home-made weapons. The militia retreated but as they left the men could hear them swearing that they would return. There was no way out of Nyarubuye now. All of the roads and the mountain tracks were crawling with Interahamwe. The militia returned some days later. This time they had the army and police with their guns and grenades.

Flora noticed that the leader of the group was none other than Sylvestre Gacumbitsi. In his car there were several policemen and a whole pile of machetes. She saw Gacumbitsi hand out the weapons. After that there was chaos. The soldiers moved in first and began to shoot; the bows and arrows were no use against guns. People were running everywhere. After the first lot of killing the militias went through finishing people off with machetes. Flora saw Gacumbitsi giving them their orders. A militiaman attacked her. She thought she recognized his face and she begged for mercy. But he just shouted at her and brought the machete down on her head. Flora collapsed and felt more bodies falling on top of her.

All day the military, the police and the Interahamwe were chasing people around and killing them. They hunted them down in rooms and in the fields around the church and inside the building itself. When they had killed everyone, or so they thought, Gacumbitsi's gang left. But underneath the mounds of corpses lay survivors, including Flora. For a week and a half she hid under the bodies, venturing out at night to try to find water, and then returning to her grim hiding place for the day. She could not remember just how long it was before a small boy came and brought some RPF soldiers who took her to hospital.

Now she had this endless pain in her head and she had dreams about the massacre all the time. Flora did not know where her family was and had no idea where she would go when her wounds healed. But of all the things about the massacre what she cannot believe is that Gacumbitsi himself actually came and directed the killing of the people. He was their Bourgmestre and he had organized the killing. Even his refusing to help them she could understand. He might have been afraid himself. But to go and tell the others to kill people. This was something terrible.

As Flora was finishing her story, sitting in the bright morning sunshine outside the clinic, a man came up and sat beside her. I recognized Silas, one of the escorts we had met on the previous night returning from Nyarubuye. 'I was there too. I was at Nyarubuye,' he said. 'I hid in the thick bushes nearby and saw the killing and I saw Gacumbitsi. He was giving out the weapons and telling his men to finish people off. He helped to finish some people off himself. I saw him.'

Silas offered to take us to Gacumbitsi's house. It was on the road south, on the way to Tanzania. Perhaps we would find something there, maybe some photographs of the Bourgmestre or some documents.

Barely half an hour later we were standing in the ransacked living-room of Sylvestre Gacumbitsi. Furniture and clothing were strewn everywhere. Sticks of chalk had been spilled on the floor and now formed a fine white powder that rose up in little clouds when we walked. There were piles of old letters in French. All seemed to have been written by one of Gacumbitsi's children to friends at school. The content was mundane. 'How are you these days? I am very well. I am studying hard ...'

Above the fireplace was a citation from Pope John Paul II. It was the routine blessing of the house usually purchased as a gift in Rome and familiar to most Catholics. Close by was a sacred heart lamp and near that some photographs of the Bourgmestre. Gacumbitsi was a big man, tall and broad with a closely trimmed beard and handsome, confident face.

In one of the photographs he is seen as a devoted family man, one baby in his arms, and his wife and three other children standing beside him. In another he is standing next to a cow that is apparently being presented to him by another man. There was something unusual about this photograph. The man who is giving the cow looks dejected, as if he wanted to be anywhere but in this picture. Silas explained that the man was a Tutsi he knew. He thought the man was probably dead by now. On Gacumbitsi's orders they had lined people up along the roadway and killed them, and Silas thought this man might have been caught trying to escape.

In the courtyard of the house we found a communion chalice, looted presumably at Nyarubuye. Nearby was Gacumbitsi's party membership card. The heat had melted the laminated plastic but the writing was still legible. The card had been given to the Bourgmestre to allow him to attend the last major party conference the previous year. There he would have heard the late President Habyarimana rail against the RPF and pledge resistance to power-sharing with them.

Beyond the high green hedge that surrounded the house were Gacumbitsi's plantations, heavy now with the smell of avocados, bananas and coffee. The plantations stretched over several acres and suggested that the Bourgmestre was a very prosperous man. In a few weeks it would be time to harvest the avocados. But the owner had fled and his labourers were either refugees or dead. The harvest would simply rot away.

SPIRITUAL DAMAGE

Nairobi, October 1995

Providing coverage of the massacre in Rwanda left its mark on the
news teams involved; it also forced them to ask themselves
questions which were often difficult to answer.

We had been looking forward to this moment for weeks. We
were sitting in an air-conditioned room in Nairobi, sipping
cold drinks and waiting for our first hot food in what seemed
like an age. There were four of us: myself, cameraman Glenn
Middleton, sound recordist Tony Wende and producer Rizu
Hamid. All the way down to the Burundi border by road, and
on the flight to Kenya, we had speculated about the joys of hot
baths and soft beds. The last stage of our journey out of Rwanda
had been nerve-racking. Through roadblock after roadblock
manned by drunken Hutu militiamen, Rizu had pleaded our
case. No, we were not Belgians she told them. We were not supporters of the Rwandan Patriotic Front (RPF). We were not
'enemies of the people'. A few of the machete-wielding thugs
didn't believe us. Some dangled their grenades through the
open windows of our vehicles. Others were simply nervous,
wondering if the rebels had entered the area yet. Most of these
people had been involved in the murder of their Tutsi neighbours. Tutsi men, women and children had died at roadblocks
like this. Now and again the smell of the dead would drift out
across the warm air of the afternoon. Somewhere in the bushes
were rags and bones and withering flesh. I thanked God for
Rizu's calm, deliberate explanations. Only when we reached the
other side of the border and stopped to check the vehicles did I
notice that my hands were shaking.

Now, as we sat waiting for lunch in Nairobi, far from the

darkness of those roads, we found ourselves wordless. There was none of the banter which had kept us going in the previous weeks. We stared at the menu, although we had already ordered. We gazed out of the window, looked around at the other guests, stared at the cutlery and tapped our fingers on the tabletop. It was Glenn who tried to break the silence. 'Some bloody place – I mean, can you believe the place? Unreal. Bloody Rwanda.' And then, for the first time in the three years I had known him, Glenn's eyes filled up with tears. He looked away from us, back out over the buildings and the traffic. And then he got up and left the table and went to his room. I tried to talk to the others about how we might structure our film but, in spite of myself, I found my voice thickening, my eyes starting to swim. Looking around me I noticed that Tony and Rizu had also started to weep. Then one by one we left the table, leaving our food uneaten as the waiters looked bemused at our sudden departure.

Looking back on that moment, I have come to believe that, in its own painful way, it represented the truest expression of the Rwandan experience. Ours was an inarticulacy born of sorrow, fear and incomprehension. Each of us had experienced war and killing before, but in Rwanda we had stepped into a place in which all previous experience of death and conflict paled into insignificance. Here the journalism of objective assessment and rational comparisons meant nothing. To this day I am at a loss to describe what it was really like. That smell. On your clothes, on your skin. For weeks afterwards, lifting a glass to your lips or sitting down to eat, it could come flashing back. This was not something I could convey with words or photographs or film. Set against the vastness of the evil of genocide, journalism was at best a limited vehicle of expression, at worst a crude and inadequate tool. For how, really, do you convey that sense of evil felt as a physical presence? To walk at night across an overgrown courtyard strewn with the rotting dead, to have to watch every step because in the long grass there are the decapitated heads of the murdered. Or to listen to a fourteen-year-old boy describe how he took a club and beat his elderly neighbour's head to a pulp and then, cheered on by soldiers, moved through a field meting out the same death to other neighbours lying tied up on the ground.

The experience still leaves me struggling for adequate words. To borrow Yeats' phrase, I have started to wonder if the unhinged world I travelled through represented a 'pity beyond all telling'. I have tried to tell the story in film and print but I have begun to accept that the ordinary language of journalism has failed me. Even though, thanks to the director, David Harrison, we produced a powerful film for *Panorama*, it could only intimate part of the reality. I had a similar feeling when I opened Gilles Peress' book of photographs, *The Silence*. It offers us a striking series of images in black and white; the landscape of the genocide. We can see the dead and their terrible twisted features. We can see the killers and the refugees and the towns and villages where the slaughter took place. But, for me, Rwanda is a country whose spiritual landscape is framed in images and memories that even the most brilliant photography cannot capture. Perhaps the only definitive testament can come from a survivor, a Rwandan Primo Levi who will give voice to that for which I can still find no words.

Although I felt a deep sense of journalistic inadequacy, the Rwandan genocide brought me more kudos than any other story I have ever covered. This has left me with lingering feelings of guilt. Perhaps it is an inescapable part of the territory. If you operate in the zones of misery, the sense of being somehow an exploiter is never far away. I have had people call me a vulture and there are times when my own reactions have made me feel ashamed. I can remember attending a mass funeral where the families of the dead were almost knocked over by jostling cameramen and photographers. One part of me was sickened by the spectacle, the other busy ensuring that my own cameraman was able to keep standing and focus on the grieving relatives. At the final stage of the process we compress the horror into minutes of television film or assemble it between the covers of a book. There are people who believe that by packaging the horror in such a way we increase the distance between the subject and the audience. This thought flickered through my mind when I first picked up Peress' book but, on a second viewing, I believe he has illuminated, not softened the horror.

If the story is to be told, if we are to give witness, what can we do but focus, switch on the record button and let the tape or film run? This is especially true of Africa, where a journalism of passion and involvement is essential. We must not report countries like Rwanda as if they were demented theme parks, peopled by savages doomed to slaughter each other in perpetuity. Too much of the reporting of Africa has been conditioned by a view of its people as an eternally miserable smudge of blackness stretching across the decades, from the Congo in the sixties to Rwanda in the nineties. In the aftermath of the Rwandan genocide there was far too much reliance on tired clichés about ancient tribal hatreds. The fact that this was an act of systematically planned mass murder, a final solution of monstrous proportions, was too often lost in the rush to blame the catastrophe on the old bogey of tribalism. This was not just lazy journalism, it was an insult to the nearly one million dead.

Since returning from Rwanda, I have heard many smug voices decrying the savage Africans and their 'lost continent'. Such talk is easy, but it ignores the truth of vast numbers of good, decent people working against odds that would drive the average Westerner over the edge in a matter of days. It also conveniently ignores the role of Europeans, men of civilization and learning, in fermenting division and resentment across the

continent of Africa. It should never be forgotten that the identity card system which allowed the Hutu extremists to round
up their opponents with such ease was introduced by the
colonialists. Or that it was German troops who tutored
Rwandan peasants in the arts of massacre in the last century.

In writing this article, I find myself walking away from the
task again and again. It is not a subject I wish to face. I make
coffee. Go for a walk. Listen to the radio. I live in Asia now and
Rwanda is a place I left behind me. Now that I sit down to
write, however, the old questions have come. They are not
questions that find their way into the average news report or
documentary. Questions about good and evil and life and
death. I remember, on my way into Rwanda, meeting a colleague who described it as a 'spiritually damaging' place. At
the time, his remark puzzled me. Now I understand it only
too well. Although I had covered acts of evil, I had managed
to retain a belief in a world where the triumph of evil was
prevented by an ultimate force for good. That belief has disappeared. It was whittled away in Kigali, Butare, Rusomo,
Nyarabuye and all the other acres of suffering where the genocide was acted out.

With the help of counselling and friends I have managed to
put my bad dreams behind me. What has not gone, what may
never go, is a deep feeling of sorrow for all the poor ruined
humanity I encountered in those months of spring last year.

After editing the film I took a long holiday in Canada,
anxious to remove myself from Rwanda and anything to do
with Africa. One afternoon, driving through the mountains
outside Vancouver, I switched on the radio to hear a Canadian
reporter describing the death by cholera of thousands of Hutu
refugees. At one point the Canadian reporter broke down as
she described how bodies were being piled on to trucks.

On this occasion the world did react. Unlike the genocide,
when most of the world was looking the other way, the

cameras were on hand to record the crisis. There was a massive humanitarian aid effort and endless political speeches. Although I sympathized with the dead and dying, I felt angry with the world for caring so much now when it had cared so little about the genocide. The Americans, who had bickered over the funding of armoured vehicles which might have been used to protect the beleaguered Tutsi population, now rushed to organize air drops.

The second act of the great Rwandan tragedy was played out in full view of the media. The disaster was a much easier story to cover than the genocide. It was, on the face of it, very simple: refugees flee for their lives and end up starving and dying. For the US television networks in particular, this had powerful resonance: there were unmistakable echoes of Ethiopia and the 'Feed the World' campaigns of the eighties. For a few weeks, the story dominated the bulletins. And then, when the body count dropped, they all packed up and moved on. Most people I met in America that summer had no notion that the catastrophe in the camps was the direct consequence of one of the worst acts of genocide since the Holocaust. It was as if the memory of mass slaughter was being buried under a fresh mound of dead bodies.

I cannot pretend that my work made any tangible difference to the lives of those who survived the genocide, or that it influenced governments to change their policies and care about Rwanda. The Panorama film was well received by the critics but attracted a small audience. I received a few letters from people who said they'd been moved by our film, and one from a man who said he was sick and tired of watching blacks killing each other. There wasn't a scintilla of political reaction. Our disclosure that the perpetrator of one of the worst massacres was now running food distribution in a UN camp was met with a deafening silence. To the best of my knowledge he is still enjoying the protection of the United Nations. As a diplomat friend of mine put it, 'It's all very upsetting but what possible sense would it make for us to get involved in a faraway dispute in which we have no part? It might make emotional sense but not politically.'

Six months before the genocide, I had an argument with a BBC colleague during the annual review of the year programme on Radio 4. I was warning of the possibility of a disaster somewhere in central Africa. I wrongly imagined that the source of the problem might be Mobutu's Zaire, where ethnic unrest had been bubbling in the Shaba region. 'Why,' my colleague asked, 'should we spend so much time reporting on tribal disputes in obscure African countries?' I was taken aback by the question, believing that it represented a narrow view of the world. I was unable to convince her otherwise at that time.

Now that I have sifted through my emotions and thoughts about Rwanda, the answer seems terribly simple. I will care about what happens in remote African countries because Rwanda has taught me to value life in a way that I never did before. The ragged peasants who died and those who did the killing belong to the same human family as I do. This may be a troubling kinship but I cannot reject it.

To witness genocide is to feel not only the chill of your own mortality, but the degradation of all humanity. I am not worried if this sounds like a sermon. I do not care if there are those who dismiss it as emotional and simplistic. It is the fruit of witness. Our trade may be full of imperfections and ambiguities but if we ignore evil we become the authors of a guilty silence.

——————— Part Three ———————

ASIA

ASIA

THE CULT OF DEATH

Tokyo, March 1995

A nerve gas attack on the Tokyo Underground system killed eleven people and injured thousands of others. The police blamed members of a religious sect which believed the end of the world was nigh.

Takuhashi Kazumasa spent most of his working life on the underground railways. His colleagues say he was a hard-working family man; at the age of fifty, he would have been looking forward to retirement from his job as assistant station master on the Underground. In the official photograph, he appears as a stocky bluff man with a wide smile and bright eyes; a man popular with his colleagues and the civil servants who travelled with him on the Underground every morning. Some time after eight o'clock on a busy Monday last week, Takuhashi Kazumasa spotted some liquid which had spilled on to the train floor. Being the diligent man he was, he immediately mopped up the fluid. Within minutes Takuhashi Kazumasa was lying dead on the platform.

Across Tokyo similar scenes were being repeated. Men and women were staggering out of trains struggling for the open air of the above ground, gasping for breath. Many of them were vomiting and rubbing ferociously at their eyes. Here, in one of the most sophisticated, cosmopolitan and technically advanced cities in the world, human beings were writhing and convulsing like creatures possessed.

As word of the disaster spread through the city something close to a sense of group shock overtook the huge population of commuters who travel in and out of Tokyo every day from the vast suburbs around the city. When I walked among commuters that evening, I sensed something approximating to disbelief. As one woman, a civil servant in the Foreign Ministry put it to me, 'This kind of thing we expect to happen in the Third World, maybe to happen in India, or even among the Arabs and the Israelis, but not to us here in Japan.'

Before long police sources were telling us that the culprits were the religious sect Aum Shinrikyo or Path of Supreme Truth, led by a bearded, plump guru, Shoko Asahara. As befits the modern cult leader, Mr Asahara is driven around in a Rolls-Royce limousine and requires that all his followers donate their assets to the cult. He preaches that the world will end in 1997, and his followers have a predilection for kidnapping critics and cult members who try to leave.

One of the most popular group rituals involves immersion in warm water for hours on end. Or, for those especially keen to prove their loyalty to the guru, there is the opportunity to spend up to a month at a time sitting underground in a tiny darkened room.

Now, none of this is all that extraordinary in the strange world of cult rituals. No, what set Mr Asahara and his 10 000 or so followers aside was their activities in the field of chemistry. We now know that they stored enough dangerous chemicals to kill millions of people and they had the potential to produce enough sarin nerve gas to make serious inroads into the population of Japan.

I visited the group's headquarters, the so-called Death Factory, on several occasions this week. The collection of large white buildings stands out from several miles away on the undulating farmland beneath Mount Fuji. The members of Aum Shinrikyo whom I met, those who were not busy arguing with the police, were decidedly unwelcoming. The sight of our cameras produced shoves and pushes and abuse, all very un-Buddhist. Most of the young men wore strange white skull caps out of which protruded electric wires. These were connected to their ears by means of masking tape so that they resembled, well I'm not actually sure what they resembled, they were just very, very strange.

But let us not be deluded by the weird and wacky images which emerged during the course of this story. What we were witnessing, if the evidence is to be believed, was something very terrible. A man possessed by an apocalyptic obsession, with the charisma to draw thousands of followers, had apparently decided to create and use a weapon of mass destruction. Our century has seen many dark figures whose hatred for humanity has expressed itself in destruction. From Hitler to Charles Manson they have all of them managed to lure and mobilize the disillusioned, the marginalized, the socially outcast. The Italian writer Primo Levi called them monsters who use beautiful words.

If Asahara and the cult are guilty of the gas attack and plotting mass destruction, and one has to point out that they protest innocence, then the world has crossed a frightening moral threshold. Here, for the first time, we will have encountered a terrorist group which both possesses the technology of mass destruction and the willingness to use it.

Governments and armies have used gas before, from World War One to the Iran-Iraq conflict, but governments are generally amenable to diplomatic and military pressure. Terrorist organizations, as a rule, do not obey the Geneva Convention. I am certain that the lesson on the Tokyo Underground will have been picked up by fanatics across the world. The terrible death of Takuhashi Kazumasa is a warning to us all.

SOUND OF THE CITY

Hong Kong, May 1995

The cacophony of Hong Kong and its population's relentless quest for wealth can sometimes prove intolerable, inducing a desire to get away from it all.

I am drowning in noise, the all-obliterating waves of noise that rip the morning asunder, for this is Hong Kong where the anthems of the piledrivers, the traffic, the demolition squads attack the ears. Will I ever come to accept this siren song of a city that must endlessly reinvent itself, expanding up and up in long concrete fingers, making room for more and more people, and all the noise they bring with them? This is a trading post of the nuclear age, the ultimate world of the here and now.

Hong Kong is two years away from Chinese rule and everybody I meet is rushing to make what they can. In Hong Kong the sound of money flows out of smart shops and back-alley noodle stalls, and you hear it in the voices of the hotel bellboys, in the declamatory horns of the taxis. How I long for the sound of rooks in an Irish wood or the bark of a sheepdog in a distant valley, or, favourite of all sounds, river water on a summer evening when the salmon ripple and splash.

Instead I am immersed here in the philosophy of the tangible. For what is Hong Kong's endless roar about, if not the voice of a people who are questing after the material, the here and now, the what can be grasped and banked or spent before 1997? It is a philosophy born of a refugee culture, defined and shaped in a space too small for the millions who live here. The people who flooded in as stateless immigrants down the decades knew the meaning of poverty and dispossession. Is it any wonder they have given this city a voice that roars determination?

Enterprise here has acted as a magnet for the world's money, and for the armies of young financiers, whose loud confident voices fill the bars and restaurants of Wanchai and Central. Now, understand, I do not believe there is anything intrinsically wrong with any of this monetary questing and hoarding, this obsession with temporal riches. But, sometimes, like yesterday, when I need to escape the sound of money, I board the ferry, heading out across the boat-swamped harbour, past the Chinese merchant ships with their patient red flags, and the American aircraft carrier, foglights translucent in the mist, until I reach the island of Lantau.

Here, among the foreign tourists and the Chinese pilgrims, I lean into the greenness and silence. There is mist here, a blanket of slowly spreading grey which wraps itself around the music of the monks, and allows only the smallest spaces for other human interruptions.

I climb the steep stairway to where the giant bronze Buddha sits, and, at the very top, among the tired pilgrims, I try to look back across the harbour towards Hong Kong, and strain to hear something of that loud voice. But it is lost to me, blissfully drowning in the sound of woodpigeons among thick trees and the murmur of children, disappearing down forest paths into the immense quiet of the afternoon.

FATHER JOE'S OUTING

South Pacific, June 1995

Joining a group of children on an outing in the South Seas
brought back memories of long-gone summers.

It was darkening now, and a fat moon rose behind the island,
showering the shallows with light. Needles of phosphorescence
ignited in the wake of the boat as it moved in towards the
beach. Father Joe had cut the engine, and one of the island boys
stood on the bow, poling us into the smooth waters near the
shoreline. Behind us the Calvados Islands stretched off towards
New Guinea, and beyond that the great immensity of Asia.

An hour earlier we crossed the last great coral reef before
Neimoa, Father Joe steering carefully while an islander whispered directions in his ear. No matter how many times he had
crossed this jagged, obstacle course, the priest wanted the
voice of an islander in his ear, whispering the turns of the
wheel like an 'Our Father'. And then we were clear into the lee
of the Calvados where a marlin leapt across our bows and the
schools of flying fish chased across the waves, while the children cheered and sang: 'Five little hungry frogs sitting on a
great big log, eating all the delicious bugs, yum, yum.' Now in
the shallows one of them had seen a shark. It lay straight ahead
in the shaky light-beams of Father Joe's ancient torch, a small
sandshark dozing in the white sands of the shallows.

The three children were on holiday with Father Joe; he was
a friend of their mother, and they had begged him to rescue
them from the boredom of the summer holidays. The youngest
was called Mitchey, and his two sisters began to tease him. 'That
shark will eat you Mitchey,' they cried. But Mitchey wasn't
bothered. He knew the sandshark only cared about fish.

We made the last kilometres of the journey on a small fishing skip. The island smell, ozone, hibiscus, coconut, sweet wild grass, flowed toward us on the night breeze and Mitchey, who had spoken all the way down about leaping on to the beach, fell fast asleep, and was carried on to the sand by his eldest sister.

Over the next three days, I watched the children as they followed Father Joe from one end of the island to the other. They teased Mitchey relentlessly and then cuddled him; they pretended to steal his food, and then fed him with toffees. In the mornings, they would run diving into the crystal waters, hooting and shrieking, splashing each other until, exhausted from the play, they would fall on the hot sand and sing of the small frogs, or 'Frère Jacques', or tunes of the South Seas unknown to me.

When I left them, watching their smiling faces growing ever more distant, as the boat began its inexorable journey out of Eden, I felt a pang for all my own summers past and gone, and for the adult life with all its trials that even now was slowly swimming towards them.

TRANS-SIBERIAN ATTACK

Ulan Bator, June 1995

With the collapse of Communism, Mongolia was forced to fend for itself – and found it hard to cope.

About an hour north of Ulan Bator, the big herdsman stormed into the carriage and headed straight for where I was sitting. He wore a rough cloak fastened around the waist by a piece of rope and on his feet a pair of sturdy leather boots. I was to make the intimate acquaintance of these formidable items of footwear in just a few seconds for, as I looked away briefly, the herdsman drove his right foot, with considerable force, into my knee. In other words, he kicked me, hard.

I gasped with surprise, too taken aback and too small to mount a counter-attack. Getting into a fight with a Mongolian herdsman on the Trans-Siberian Express is not recommended, so I looked around for the train guard who had been assigned as our guide. I need not have worried. He materialized from the toilet in seconds, and, although much smaller in height and weight, launched a ferocious assault on the herdsman. He punched, kicked and swore. In a few minutes, the big man was subdued and blubbering. The train was stopped, and he was ejected into the wilderness, miles from any station or apparent human settlement.

The other passengers, mostly traders ferrying electrical goods between Moscow and Ulan Bator, took all this in their stride. In fact, most ignored the action altogether. When I inquired as to why the guard had responded in, well, what some might call an extreme fashion, he told me that this was Mongolia, and they had rough ways of dealing with trouble-makers. It seems the big herdsman thought I was a Russian, and the Russians, once the economic mainstay of Mongolia, are now despised by many, having abandoned the country that was once their effective colony, and retreated with their money and soldiers back to the motherland.

That afternoon, as the train rattled and rolled across the vast hilly terrain that stretched north in a carpet of spring green, I watched teams of horsemen, appearing out of the emptiness like ghosts, chasing in front of them the herds of horses. Some carried long poles with which they roped in the wilder of the animals and, behind them, in the wake of the horses and their fearsome-looking masters, rose trails of dust, galloped up into the air by a hundred pounding hooves. From the window, the plains of Mongolia looked forbidding, bleak, endless.

I wondered what would become of the herdsman. Was he lost now, wandering hopelessly with the night coming on, and the temperature, even in late May, sinking to freezing? I thought back to what somebody had told me in Ulan Bator before we left. I had been talking about the economic hardship which had followed the Russian withdrawal, its appalling effect on children, and the rise of social problems like alcoholism and violence. 'Yes that's true,' he said, 'but always remember, you are talking about people who once conquered China, who very nearly managed to conquer Europe. They are tough. Don't underestimate them.'

For all that I found it hard to see the image of Genghis Khan and his Golden Horde reflected in the eyes of the hard-pressed citizens of Ulan Bator. There was a misery about the people, a doleful expression, which spoke of lives lived on the margins: a struggle to feed themselves and their families, to keep warm in freezing winters, to find jobs and get their children to school, when the money which sustained the state has drained out of the country, north across the border into Siberia.

What is saddest, is the sense of how a people's pride in

themselves, in their heritage and ancestry, is being worn down in the face of economic troubles. There is a fierce sensitivity to criticism or investigation by outsiders. When we filmed groups of street children begging, we were chased by groups of angry women. 'Stop showing the world the bad side of Mongolia,' they cried.

The government is under pressure from the world's financial institutions to trim public spending, and most diplomats agree that it is doing the best it can under difficult circumstances. But with millions of roubles still owed to Russia, a vastly underdeveloped infrastructure and rising unemployment, Mongolia will find it hard to return to the days of imperial glory.

Perhaps the train conductor was right, perhaps the herdsman really did believe I was a Russian, and that kick in the leg was his only way of hitting back for all the shame and frustration of life in post-Soviet Mongolia. In the long run I suspect his wounded pride was a much more severe wound than my bruised leg.

A CITY'S DESTRUCTION

Kabul, October 1995

The capital city of Afghanistan was being gradually destroyed by the long-running civil war which had taken the lives of more than a million people.

We had just travelled a mile along the road when a loud whooshing noise swept over the car and our driver, Amir Shah, reached forward, grasped his Koran, and kissed the holy book. 'Rockets,' he said, 'but I think they're going out, not coming in.' I was indescribably pleased with this piece of information and then I remembered that indisputable law of military science: outgoing attracts incoming. 'Don't worry my friend, don't worry,' said Amir Shah as we rattled along the road towards the government's front-line position.

On either side of us was a wasteland of demolished buildings and rusting vehicles. On those few houses still standing we could see the deranged artwork of the AK47, its brute patterns sprayed across the walls like a cave painting from some doomed civilization. Here and there, there were larger holes punched by rockets and then, in the middle of the road, a huge crater caused by a Scud missile during the last battle for Kabul.

The southern suburbs of this city give a new definition to the word desolation, yet people still live in these ghostly streets, hiding from the war in a maze of crumbling buildings. An occasional face peers out from the grey devastation and glances fleetingly at the foreigners who have appeared out of nowhere. Amir Shah has travelled this road so many times that he is frequently recognized.

At a government base in the ruins of a school, the Commander greeted us warmly and insisted that we stay for tea. Amir Shah hovered about making introductions, seeking permission to film, talking and smiling; a perfect mixture of humility and steely determination. The Commander insisted that I sit, eat and say grace with him. His gunners were busy launching rocket and howitzer fire into the Taleban positions up the road. 'Why don't you join us for the fight, come and fight on our side?' he said. I told the Commander that I was a soft city boy, I would be too much of a hindrance. By the time Amir Shah had finished translating, the Commander and his men were laughing loudly.

As we left, the guns started up again and more high explosives flew in the direction of the Taleban line. We could hear them landing in the valley a few kilometres away. The sound was like a huge door being slammed, followed by clouds of white smoke rising in the clear light of the autumn morning. And so we drove on towards the front and the key government position at the old presidential palace.

Here, Afghanistan's former communist rulers and their Soviet puppet masters had lived in grand style, believing that their weapons and organization could keep the ragged Mujahedeen at bay. They were wrong, and the place is a fitting monument to their folly. The palace, or what is left of it, is constructed in what I can only describe as Afghan Gothic: a confusion of turrets and yellow brick. It is one of the most dangerous places in the country. The Taleban fighters across the valley regularly send rockets and mortar shells flying into the ruins.

As we drove up the side of the mountain towards the palace, Amir Shah announced that we were now in full view of the Taleban gunners. 'Then get the hell back down out of here,' I exclaimed. 'Yes, Mr Keane, I think you are right,' he replied, slamming the car into reverse and heading straight back down the hill. Beyond us in the valley a shell landed, its smoke cloud like a warning.

At the bottom of the hill, young fighters lounged around

unconcerned by the possibility of bombardment. They were happy to be filmed. Almost everybody on the government side is camera-aware. Afghanistan's fifteen-year war has attracted countless camera crews down the years.

The commanding officer wanted to take us out to the forward trenches occupied by his artillery spotters, the men who pinpoint the enemy positions for the gunners. They occupy a sort of advanced front-line between their own main forces and the enemy. Here we would be able to see the Taleban clearly and they presumably could see us.

'Come with us. Come on,' said the Commander. He was a huge bear of a man with long, black, curly hair and a thick beard. Other men who clustered around him were clearly awed by his presence. 'It will only take twenty minutes to get you out there and back,' he said. I looked at cameraman Fred Scott, a calm, cool Californian who had covered the last major battle for Kabul. 'I don't much see the point,' said Fred.

He confirmed the doubts in my own mind that the front line was scary enough without pushing our luck out across the floor of the valley. At such times I find it healthy to visualize people I love and the landscapes of home: mountains, green fields, rivers full of fish. We all quickly agreed that life was too sweet to play poker with and so we climbed back into Amir Shah's old taxi and drove as fast as its engine could carry us back towards Kabul and the comforting presence of other civilians.

Now, as I write, the evening prayers are echoing across the dusk and occasionally the holy words are interrupted by shell-fire. Another day of war in Afghanistan is coming to an end.

RAJANA DEVI'S LAST MOMENTS

Colombo , December 1995

The suicide bomb was one of the tactics used
by the Tamil Tiger rebels of Sri Lanka in their campaign
for a separate homeland.

Colombo on a sweltering monsoon Saturday. A Buddhist monk
beats his drum and chants a mantra for the dead. Crowds of
onlookers have gathered along the railway track. A goat is nos-
ing among the piles of rubbish and chewing. Policemen direct
traffic away from the scene. I walk towards the barrier and pass
a small shoe. I think it is a size three woman's shoe. I know
because my wife takes size three. There is the smallest smear of
blood inside the shoe.

Further on I see rubble and the light of a photographer's
flashbulb. On the ground are some things I would rather not
describe in detail, but among them the torso and head of a
young woman who has blown herself up. Parts of the people
she killed are also lying around. I learn later that her name is
Rajana Devi and that she was in her late twenties. She first came
to the attention of the police in the late eighties when she was
arrested in eastern Sri Lanka in the area around Batticaloa.
Rajana Devi was a suicide bomber, one of the Tamil Tigers' élite.

On that hot, sunny morning, she had got up, strapped on a
bomb and then walked along the seafront, the fresh ocean
breezes in her face, before turning left in the direction of the
army headquarters. Here, her colleague had attempted to
breach security but had only succeeded in detonating his
bomb at a sentry hut. She, we are told, saw this and fled in
panic towards the railway junction a short distance away. She

would have passed through busy crowds, people drawn to the area, as they always are in Sri Lanka, by the sound of the explosion. At some point, looking into the faces of these people, she would have pressed the button, or pulled the cord, and blown herself and those around her to pieces.

I thought of her a great deal in the days that followed, struggling to understand the choice she had made, the wilful obliteration of her own life and those of the innocent people standing around her. Even though I have seen men from my own country slowly starve themselves to death for their cause, I found Rajana Devi's apocalypse incomprehensible.

Perhaps if I had simply read about it in a newspaper, it would have been easier, but to see her remains, and then the gory photographs produced afterwards by the army. Let me just say that it confronted my capacity for understanding.

About a week later as I was preparing to travel into Tamil Tiger territory in the East, the area where Rajana Devi had first come to the security forces' attention, her image came back to me again. The soldiers at the last army checkpoint were nervous. They had been attacked the night before. We were travelling on at our own risk, they said. The road that stretched ahead represented danger and mayhem to them. I did not explain that I thought the Tamil Tigers would be unlikely to attack us. Even the rawest recruits are lectured on the importance of the foreign media.

It was a beautiful, almost cloudless morning and the waving fronds of the sugar cane appeared like the tentacles of anemones deep under the sea. We drove on for nearly an hour across the plain, our nervousness seeping away as people began to appear, walking along the road, and working in the fields. The sugar cane gave way to rice paddies on whose watery surface the sun glinted. And then, as if from the air, a group of guerrillas appeared from a clump of palm trees and bushes on the right-hand side of the road. They did not wave us down, but, in any event, we stopped, anxious to speak to and film them.

There were seven of them and they were all teenagers. Their commander was a sixteen-year-old boy. All wore cyanide capsules around their necks, enough poison in each glass vial to kill several men, they assured me. I asked them why they were fighting. 'Because the Tamils were getting no justice in Sri Lanka,' one of them answered. But they were being offered devolution by the government, why not accept that?, I asked.

'We want our own state. We have our state. Why should we accept anything else?' came the response. Everyone spoke with soft voices. They were unfalteringly polite and all assured me that they would not hesitate to kill themselves, and presumably anybody else they were told to kill, in the struggle for Tamil Eelam, their homeland.

They took me to a bungalow hidden away behind a high wall. Groups of older men, carrying briefcases and papers, sat in the shade. A meeting of some sort had just finished. I followed the boy-soldiers into a small room where a stocky moustached man was sitting at a table, flanked by two exceptionally tough-looking bodyguards. This man was Commander Karikalan, number two in the Tigers' political structure and chief of the eastern military region. For the next half hour he again patiently answered my questions, and again reassured me that people were willing to die for the cause. In fact, when it came to recruiting suicide bombers, there was always a rush to sign up for the job. They were determined to fight and die for a permanent Tamil homeland, he said.

Now there are those who tell you that suicide bombers are people whose families have suffered more than most at the hands of the security forces. Still others tell you that they are brainwashed by the Tigers. But none of what I heard behind rebel lines or from the government side, came close to explaining Rajana Devi's choice on that monsoon morning in

Colombo. I am left with the imagining of her last seconds; of the sound of voices and traffic, and the curious expressions of those around her, and whatever thought, who knows what it was, that went through her mind before the blinding flash of oblivion.

FAREWELL HONG KONG

Hong Kong, February 1996

**During the last months of British rule, the people of the colony
tried to come to terms with the fact that, come June 1997, the
Chinese would take control.**

The great imperial jumble sale has begun. In elegant apartment
buildings all over Hong Kong, discreet little notices are starting
to appear 'For sale: table and two chairs and assorted house-
hold effects,' is just one of many spotted recently as Britain's
imperial civil servants begin packing up for home ahead of
1997. Whole forests of rattan wood furniture are being
uprooted from comfortable living rooms to start new lives in
the homes of Chinese families who either do not have the
right of abode in Britain or, much more likely, are making too
much money in Hong Kong to want to leave.

In my own apartment block, my wife recently became the
heiress to a vast collection of plants, bequeathed to her by a
British couple. The husband had spent eighteen years in the
colonial police force and the family's four children had grown
up in Hong Kong. Naturally he was sad to be leaving but
accepted the reality. Hong Kong was part of China and a Brit in
a Chinese police uniform was a non-starter.

The process of localization, or Chinification as many are
starting to call it, is well underway. In simple terms this
involves the retiring of existing British civil servants, with generous golden handshakes, and the appointment, in their place,
of Hong Kong Chinese. How many of the new appointees will
continue in their posts once Beijing takes over is another question, however. The Communist Party has a long tradition of
making sure that the structures of government are entirely

within its control. There is no reason to believe that Hong Kong will be any different.

Naturally enough, the approach of 1997 fills the pro-democracy activists – and many of those who made their livelihood working for the British – with dread. I sat recently with Democratic leader Martin Lee in the lavishly appointed dining-room of the Hong Kong Club. This little corner of empire, with its deep carpets and armies of doormen and waiters, is close to the Legislative Council building where Lee regularly proclaims the virtues of democracy to the fury of Beijing.

Lee has told others that he is prepared for anything once 1997 comes. Some have taken this to mean that he believes there will be a purge once the take-over happens, with pro-democracy figures being despatched to labour camps. When I asked him about this, Martin Lee was surprisingly relaxed. No, he didn't expect an immediate purge. The Chinese had too much to lose if they were to be seen to crack down ruthlessly. He expected things to happen much more slowly and quietly until some day people would wake up and any sense of democracy would have disappeared.

But Lee's biggest fear, and that of many ordinary people, is that the rule of law will cease to exist after the take-over. They have only to pick up the South China Morning Post every day to read news from China of blatant violations of commercial laws, of deals broken and courts unwilling to take action. The economic boom in China has brought with it a freebooting frontier atmosphere in which it is as easy to lose one's shirt as it is to make a fortune.

In Hong Kong, where making money is the single greatest imperative, the thought that the rules which protect property and wealth might become useless fills people with mortal dread. As a Chinese friend of mine put it to me recently, 'Do you mean to say that I have worked all my life for what I have so that some country boy from up north can steal it all, just because he is wearing an official uniform? Absolutely no way.'

My friend is one of those lucky enough to have a foreign passport. With his Canadian travel document he is well placed to depart for Vancouver (known here as Hongcouver for its large Hong Kong Chinese population) should everything start to go wrong after 1997.

Most people here do not have second passports, however. And it is among the poorer sections of society that one notices the greatest sense of apprehension. This does not manifest itself in open complaining or political campaigning. Instead, the working classes of Kowloon and the vast estates beyond have begun to work harder and harder, saving up for the rainy day they fear may be just round the corner.

I have never lived anywhere where the noise of commerce, the sound of money and the rhythm of human effort was so tangible. Take a walk in the crowded streets of Causeway Bay, past the stalls selling steaming noodles, through the little alley-ways with their cobblers and antique sellers, and on into the neon glitter of Hennessy Road and you will feel the surge of energy. There are millions being made here every day. Vast piles of money finding their way into the safety of secret bank accounts that no communist official will ever be allowed to get his hands on.

Yet, in spite of the murmurings of worry and the heady rush to make hay while the sun shines, there is no real sense of an end of empire. Having watched the decline of the last white empire in South Africa, I think I have a reasonable ear for the sounds of an imperial requiem. I do not yet hear them in Hong Kong. Perhaps that is because it was never really a British colonial city in the way that Delhi was, or Cape Town. In fact there is a far greater sense of the imperial past in the older parts of Dublin than there is anywhere in Hong Kong.

The city is, and always has been, a Chinese city which, for

a period in history, became a major trading post of the British empire. But the English language has not taken root here, and neither have the sporting and cultural traditions of the mother country. British rule did provide a framework for the commercial exploitation and success of Hong Kong, but, in doing so, it merely provided an outlet for the ingrained commercial instincts of the Cantonese.

The British who are leaving seem to recognize the inevitable. One hears little whining. There is tacit acceptance, though never quite spoken, that 'We don't really belong here'. There is however an up-and-coming generation of new 'colonials'. These are the young men and women, in sharp business suits, who fill the bars and cafés, chattering incessantly into mobile phones as they discuss one huge deal after another. They bore me terribly, talking only of money and material advancement. Yet they are the new reality. These children of the investment age have come from all over the world to take their chance in Hong Kong. They work incredibly long hours and reap vast rewards. Most intend to stay on, believing that the communists will not want to kill the goose which continues to lay such large golden eggs.

I tend to think they are correct. Those who want to make money will not find themselves too much troubled by the new rulers for the time being. Rather, I agree with Martin Lee; the time to sing the dirge for the 'good old days of British rule' will probably come much later, long after the last Union Jack has fluttered on the hills overlooking Hong Kong.

ST PATRICK'S DAY
IN TAIPEI

March 1996

China was conducting a series of military exercises in the Taiwan
Strait as Irish men and women, around the world, prepared to
celebrate their national day.

Hot days, spring in the city and a warm wind is blowing in
from the East China Sea. Down on the coast, about half an
hour's flight from here, hundreds of people are packing up
their belongings and climbing on to navy ships heading away
from the islands of the Taiwan Strait where the Chinese war
machine is growling its bellicose warnings. These are long
days in Taiwan. Long days waiting for something to happen,
hoping it won't, not knowing which way the Chinese are
going to play it.

I guess you would think I would far prefer to be in Ireland
just now, celebrating our national day, the great annual feast of
our founding saint, the Roman boy abducted from Britain and
carried into slavery in the wild mountains of what was then
called Hibernia. Well, the truth is I am glad I am here in Taiwan
and not in Cork or Dublin because, call me a curmudgeon if
you will, but St Patrick's Day bores me senseless. No offence to
the long-departed saint, but this orgy of self-conscious
Irishness is not for me.

Maybe it is the memory of those awful parades of my
childhood, where we stood shivering in the March winds and
watched the grandees of the city leading float after float down
St Patrick's Street followed by the eternal ranks of goose-
pimpled majorettes with their triangles and their drums. It
was always cold and always windy, and the faces of the

Chamber of Commerce and Rotary men were always painfully serious. Everything closed down for the day and the television programmes were even more useless than usual. When we got older, there was the annual schools' rugby cup final and my school seemed to lose quite a few of them.

Win or lose, the day always ended with gallons of green beer and a long retching walk home, having been refused entrance to a disco. Green beer? A symbol of Irishness? Spare me. It always just seemed to bring an even worse hangover.

No, I would like to celebrate Irishness in a quieter way, a less public way. What I would like to be doing right now would be sitting in my small fishing boat heading out around Ardmore Head in County Waterford in the direction of Goat Island, past the wreck of the *Samson*, perched below Father Murphy's rock, the wind coming in from the south-east behind my back and the day stretching out lazily ahead in the sun, like Jimmy Maloney's old labrador in front of the fire.

I would have Jimmy with me in the boat and we would move in closer to the rocks where the cormorants stand preening and scanning the glass-green surface. Jimmy has known me since the day I was born. He also knows the coast around Ardmore like the back of his hand: every pool, every submerged rock, every twist in the wind.

As soon as we had found a calm spot in a lee of the cliffs where the gulls could wheel above us and the occasional walker might wave down, then we would sink our lines down to hang above the kelp beds where the wrasse and the pollack swim in the deep, deep green. Sooner or later Tony Gallagher's boat might come past and he would stop to chat, maybe swapping some of our fish for his shrimp, making a date to meet in Reilly's later on. If it was a fine day we would be able to see Capel Island in the distance, Capel where only goats live and where the big cod prowl in deep waters. Jimmy would tell stories and more stories and I might add a few of my own.

That night, our faces still glowing from the sea breeze, the whiff of fish still lingering on our hands however many soapy scrubbings, that night we would go to one of the village's fine watering holes: Keever's, Reilly's, Gallagher's or the Cliff Hotel and lose ourselves in talk and stout and maybe, later on, a few songs. Then the long, easy sleep that is possible in the place you love, among people who know you and care about you. That is my ideal day, my favourite Ireland.

EVERYTHING FOR SALE

Phnom Penh, March 1996

Cambodia became a democracy under the supervision of the United Nations, hoping to become the next booming Asian economy. But it still faced severe problems.

At night the musk of kerosene stoves mingles with sweat and incense, and rises out of the squatter hovels spreading over the city like the breath of an ancient plague. You can smell it on the still night air alongside the Tonlesap river, or in the backstreets that lead away from Monevong Boulevard. The streets on which the armies of the poor peddle their cigarettes, their matches and their bodies. For Cambodia is a place where you can buy almost anything or anybody. It is as corrupt and venal a place as I have ever visited and that includes some of the more wretched states of Africa.

There was a driver who told us that he procured young girls, twelve, thirteen years of age, for Chinese businessmen. It was easy he said. The mothers would come in from the countryside, from the poverty-stricken and war-battered fastness, and offer the children for sale. 'How much do they charge?' I asked. 'It depends on how poor they are,' he replied. 'Generally speaking about a hundred dollars.' The businessmen believe that sleeping with a young virgin increases their strength. 'And what happens when they are finished with these children?' I asked. 'Oh, then they become bar-girls,' the driver replied.

The bars are really brothels where beer is served and there is street after street of them in Phnom Penh. Drive along these sad streets at night and the children in their gaudy make-up and long party dresses shout and gesture from the sidewalk. Many of their customers seem to be Asian men, princes of the economic boom that will supposedly turn Cambodia into the next Asian tiger economy.

Now, I don't mean to be entirely negative; some people are getting rich in Cambodia – a few, and they are often people with close connections to the government. Take Mr Teng Bunma for example: plump, soft-spoken, a man who likes big rings and bigger cars. A man who gave one prime minister a Mercedes, another a private jet. Mr Teng Bunma is a property speculator, president of the Phnom Penh Chamber of Commerce, a man who holds a Cambodian diplomatic pass-port, whose Kalashnikov-wielding bodyguards are supplied by the Ministry of Defence.

For the record, Mr Teng Bunma wanted to assure me that he was not one of those unnamed Cambodian businessmen with links to the government whom the US State Department accuses of being involved in the heroin trade. All of his money had been legitimately earned. Mr Teng Bunma is an advocate of what have come to be called 'Asian values'. This, in his view, involves putting economic development first and human rights second. What good is it to talk about human rights if people are living in squalor, if they are living in hell?, he asks.

At first hearing that might seem like a fairly reasonable argument but, before you are tempted to swallow it whole, consider the story of Sa Kim Youern and his family of eleven. Three years ago they came back from the Thai refugee camps they had fled to, to avoid the war between the Khmer Rouge and the Vietnamese army. They came back because Cambodia, under UN supervision, was about to become a real democracy after the long years of war and Khmer Rouge terror. But three years into this new democracy they find themselves living or, more accurately, existing, in a squatter camp.

Every day at sunset the family lines up at a park close to the river and sells sugar cane from wicker baskets which the children carry on their heads. This, to supplement the twenty dollars a month their father earns as a soldier in the national army. 'I feel a sense of shame, of embarrassment, when I see my children going out like this,' he told me. 'We sit here and watch the big cars and the new motorcycles go by but, as for me, I think I'll always be a man who goes by foot,' he said.

There is a rich irony in all of this. For the land where Sa Kim Youern and his family set up their stall was created from territory given to the government by Teng Bunma. And in order to provide the ground, Teng first had to clear the area of squatters. Now the camp where Sa Kim Youern and his family live has been scheduled for development. The developers have already attempted to burn down a section of the settlement. Sa Kim and his children had to flee for their lives and rebuild in another area. He expects another fire soon and believes that he will always be a poor man and that his children will be poor.

They are supposed to be children of a new Asia, the continent that will dominate the next century, but, to me, they look like the inhabitants of a world such as Dickens might have known. A place neither of day nor of night but rather one grey eternity of struggle.

THE BABY SNATCHERS

Alice Springs, May 1996

A legal battle was underway in Australia on behalf of thousands
of Aboriginal and half-caste children who were forcibly removed
from their parents. In a systematic campaign, which continued
until the 1960s, the children were educated and given jobs
in white communities. Some never saw their homes,
or families, again.

Take the main road west out of Alice Springs through a land of
red rock and gum trees and you will eventually come to a sign
for the Mount Riddock cattle station. The sign points into the
bush and you will need a four-wheel drive vehicle to negotiate
the sandy tracks that lead off into the wilderness. Dust clouds
rise and vanish as the car churns onwards. You drive and drive
and then some more.

After several hours the trees and mountains start to blur in
the shimmering heat. You begin to understand why the
Aboriginals called this improbably vast landscape the 'Never
Never'. It is beautiful and very daunting and you definitely
don't want to get lost. There was little fear of that happening to
me. My guide was sixty-eight-year-old George Bray and for
him every track, every clump of trees, every rock represented a
deeply personal point of reference. 'This is my country, this is
where I come from,' he said.

He had told me the outline of his story during the journey.
How at the age of five he and his brother and two sisters had
been forcibly removed from their parents and sent to live in
the Alice Springs home for mixed-race children. George had
seen his parents on and off down the years, but was never
allowed to live with them again. Now as we approached the

place where he was seized and taken away he wanted to tell me the full, terrible story.

It was mid-morning when the police came, George recalled. He was playing with his brother and cousins, his parents were preparing food and collecting wood. 'The policemen were on camels and they had shotguns. They came up to my father and said they were taking us children away. I remember they told him it was government policy to take half-caste children away and give them an education. He just didn't know what to do, he looked so confused,' remembered George.

There was an argument and then George remembers his mother starting to cry and his father pleading with the police sergeant. 'But the police just grabbed us and put us on camels. I remember one of them saying, "Come here you little black so and so," when I tried to get away; and they grabbed me hard and sat me on the camel. Then as we were being taken away I looked back at the camp and all my relatives were crying and begging, and my mother was on her knees in the dust, tearing out her hair. All her children were gone, just like that.'

George was sent first to the 'Bungalow' as the Alice Springs institution was called. He remembers the children being lined up and told that their own Aboriginal spiritual beliefs were useless. 'They just went up and down the group saying, "You and you belong to the Church of England, you and you belong to the Catholics and you belong to the Methodists." They had just decided what we would be and that was it.'

Any child found speaking an Aboriginal language was flogged. Although Aboriginal men worked at the compound, chopping wood and doing odd jobs, the children were forbidden to speak to them. They were to speak English and nothing else.

Eventually George was sent to work on one of the huge white-owned cattle stations. He worked there for years, having been told that his pay was being saved. When he went into town one day to collect his money from the bank he was told that there were no savings. 'It was just slave labour; they had no intention of paying us and we didn't have any family to stand up for us.'

Although he would have been unaware of it at the time, George Bray was a victim of a racial policy that has stained the history of Australia. From the early part of the century until the late 1960s it was state policy to remove mixed-race children from their families and raise them in the white world. This was to be done through placing them in institutions or fostering them to white families.

The prevailing wisdom was that Aboriginals were a race without a future and therefore assimilation into the white world was the only option for mixed-race children. The theory held that by removing them from their Aboriginal background they would eventually see themselves as white. Their children would marry whites and ultimately through interbreeding with whites the taint of brown skin would disappear.

The victims of the policy believe it was an attempt at genocide through assimilation. 'They took away my language and my culture and my family and I feel bitter about it,' George says.

Now George and several other stolen children have launched a legal battle seeking compensation from the state. The government has set up a Commission of Inquiry into the question of stolen children in response to a growing campaign for recognition by victims of the policy. The exact number of stolen children is hard to estimate but it is thought that tens of thousands were affected.

The policy was not limited to mixed-race children. Large numbers of so-called 'Full-blood' Aboriginals were affected as well, taken away from their families in the belief that they could be 'civilized' by exposure to the white world. Yet it is among mixed-race victims that the greatest amount of damage appears to have been inflicted.

Elna Williams, now in her mid-forties, was six hours old when she was taken away from her mother. She remembers a childhood of emotional deprivation and savage beatings. 'There was a Catholic priest at this home I was in and he used to flog us and flog us for the smallest thing. I can never forget that abuse,' she says.

Allegations of emotional and physical abuse are widespread among the stolen children. Like many others who were taken away Elna found the task of becoming a parent herself an uphill struggle. With no concept of what a loving family life meant, she became an alcoholic and eventually her own children were taken away. They became wards of state under welfare laws.

'All I knew back then,' she says, 'was that I thought you had to be angry and fight all the time. A lot of us were drinking to forget, you know. You think if you drink then the pain will go away, but it doesn't.'

Now a decade sober, Elna has started to rebuild her life. Her daughter and grandson live with her and she has become actively involved in organizing support groups for stolen children. I reminded Elna of a comment by a former policeman that children were taken away for their own good; that living with Aboriginals would have meant a life of drunkenness and destitution. She laughed and shook her head. 'No way, absolutely no way,' she said, 'I'd never have grown up with all that confusion and pain if my family background hadn't been interfered with like that.'

The most striking thing about the group of stolen children I met in Alice Springs was their determination to seek out and embrace their Aboriginal heritage. Identity and belonging were central to their lives. The attempt to make them white had, it seemed to me, had the opposite effect.

One afternoon George Bray took me back to the place where he had been born, in the shade of a large and ancient gum tree. Apart from the lazy chirping of insects and a light wind brushing the grass and leaves there was silence.

One night sixty-eight years before, under a sky flecked with the silver of the southern cross, George Bray had come into the world here. As he spoke tears began to glisten in his eyes and then creep down his cheeks. 'I was born here when there was no maternity units for us and no doctors for miles around but my parents and my people were here, and now when I come and touch this tree I feel so close to them. When I hear the wind blowing through the branches it's as if I can hear a voice saying, "You belong here in this country," and nobody, nobody can take that away from me ever.'

I walked away and left George to his thoughts. When I reached the car I looked back and saw that he had placed his arms around the tree and that he was weeping and still quietly talking.

AN INDIVIDUAL CHOICE

Rangoon, May 1996

Burma's military regime was continuing to arrest supporters of the opposition leader Aung San Suu Kyi as the rest of the world debated the morality of investing in Burma.

They serve a wonderful fish curry at the English and Oriental Club: butterfish, chunks of it, smothered in a rich red sauce, reeking of cardamom, ginger and a host of secret spices from the green interior of Burma. I know this because a businessman brought me there a couple of weeks ago. But to tell you the truth, I was not really able to enjoy my curry to the full.

Don't get me wrong, the food was wonderful and the setting sublime. A cool veranda facing on to a large lake across whose surface dragonflies whirred and butterflies danced. No, there was nothing wrong with my immediate situation or indeed the company. But as the businessman, a charming and gracious person, told me about the benefits of investing in Burma, about the good lifestyle available to foreigners and about the need for dialogue and engagement with the military regime, I could not get out of my head an encounter I had had the day before. I don't know if the businessman noticed my eyes drifting away from time to time. If he did he was much too polite to say it.

You see, I was unable to put out of my head the testimony of a young man I had met the previous evening. I cannot tell you his name – that would invite an immediate reprisal against him from the military. Nor can I tell you where I met him lest the army feel inclined to act against his neighbours, punishing all because one of their number had spoken out. I say all of this because I expect we are joined today, somewhere out there in the audience, by a listener from the Burmese secret police. They are particularly avid listeners to the BBC.

What I can tell you is the story he told me. The young man was a supporter of Aung San Suu Kyi's National League for Democracy, a fact which became known to the secret police. They duly arrested him and took him to jail for interrogation. For three days he was denied food, water or sleep and questioned, non-stop.

When that did not elicit the required confession the beatings began and went on and on. The young man and his fellow prisoners were stripped naked and thrown into a single cell. They were given the barest minimum food required to keep them alive.

When one of them complained about this, all were dragged out and thrown into a pigsty and told to wash the animals and to clean up the excrement with their hands. Then the guards were given alcohol and the beatings began again, only this time they were worse. 'It was a frenzy. They beat us and beat us like animals,' the young man told me, and he showed me the welts and scars on his arms and back to prove it. Having served several years in jail he was released and warned to stay out of politics.

Now I suppose that it is possible that his wounds were self-inflicted and that he made up the entire story. It is possible, but somehow I doubt it. Burma is that kind of place. You can simply disappear into military custody without charge. You can, along with the rest of your village, be forced to take part in slave labour for the government. If you are a man living near one of the border war-zones, you could find yourself press-ganged into carrying ammunition and food supplies for the army.

When I first went to Burma last year, I thought the atmosphere reminded me a lot of South Africa during the state of emergency. I was wrong of course. Burma is much much worse. In South Africa there was a vibrant and free press, there was a legal system which frequently challenged the state, there was a trade union movement and scores of allied human rights bodies all operating with difficulty but still able to represent the interests of the oppressed. There was also a parliamentary system, albeit only for whites, coloureds and Indians, which allowed the opposition to question and denounce the excesses of the state. South Africa's then white rulers may have presided over an odious and sometimes murderous system of racial separation, but there was a part of them which wished terribly to belong to the civilized community of nations.

In Burma there is not the remotest whiff of political freedom. It is easily the most oppressive atmosphere I have ever encountered as a journalist. Whether one is talking to a taxi driver who looks frantically over his shoulder the moment Aung San Suu Kyi's name is mentioned, or a seventeen-year-old girl who has watched her elderly neighbours fall dying by the roadside during slave labour, there is a sense of a society in which ordinary people are powerless before the might of the state.

Not that this seems to impress the foreign businessmen who are now heading to Burma to invest or to set up companies. Many of them speak of the need for constructive engagement. They argue that by talking to the regime they can liberalize the situation. What's more, they say, the presence of foreigners will have a positive effect, opening up the country to new ideas. And besides, they say, economic sanctions would simply hurt the poor and not the military regime.

One American businessman told me over drinks on my last night in Rangoon that Burma was not yet ready for democracy. 'The country would fall apart,' he said. I will leave it up to you to make your own individual choice as to whether to accept these arguments or not. For me, listening to them inside Burma, it all seemed unreal.

I know that while I lunched at the English and Oriental Club, or sipped a drink with the American businessman, there were people slaving on government projects, there were political prisoners cooped up in jail, there were, very probably, people being tortured by the secret police.

Now it is possible not to know about these things, not to have heard about them. Or to know and to rationalize that they are necessary for the preservation of stability. But it is also possible to know about them and to take the view that they are wrong, an affront to our common humanity for which there can be no excuse. It is, as I said, an individual choice.

THE LADY AND THE GENERALS

Rangoon, July 1996

A year after her release from house arrest, the military authorities in Burma were still keeping a close watch on Aung San Suu Kyi.

Two short stories from a Rangoon lunch. The meal has nearly ended when she notices the elderly guest to my left struggling to remove some chillies from his food. His fingers are bent with arthritis and he wipes away ineffectually at the red peppers. Nothing is said but I am suddenly aware of her presence leaving my side and moving to where the old man is sitting. With a few deft movements of her hand the offending spices are removed. 'There you go uncle,' she smiles, 'we must be careful of your stomach.' A few minutes later when the same old man is midway through a long rambling story about Burma's struggle against the British, her secretary appears at the door. He gestures at his watch and mouths the words 'Two o'clock. Meeting with delegation.' She acknowledges the message but continues listening. I look at my watch and notice it is already two o'clock. Yet the story continues and Aung San Suu Kyi continues smiling. Names and dates from the distant past are recalled. Her secretary reappears and is starting to look a little frantic. But she will not interrupt the old man and when he finishes, Aung San Suu Kyi waits for a moment before rising from the table.

'We'll just give the delegation a bit more time at the other end. They will understand. Of course they will,' she says, her voice breaking into a laugh as we move towards the porch where the delegates are sheltering from the sheets of monsoon rain. And then, clasping her hands together and raising them to her face in a traditional Buddhist greeting, she sets forth to receive her latest visitors.

I had first met her a year before, the day after she had been released from house arrest. Back then she had been almost breathless with excitement and hope for the future. Now nearly twelve months on she seemed physically tired but still radiating confidence. This at a time when the secret policemen were rounding up her supporters and the malevolent generals of the ruling State Law and Order Restoration Council (SLORC) were denouncing her as 'sorceress', a 'snake' and 'anorexic fashion plate' in the state press.

'Oh I don't worry about that. They have called me everything under the sun. One gets quite used to it. What I am worried about is our people who are out there and who do not have the protection that I have,' she says.

Although most of our lunch had been taken up with discussing the latest political crisis it is the two exchanges with the old man that are embedded in my memory. For they represented the grace, patience and humanity which are central to any understanding of Aung San Suu Kyi. Most other political leaders of my aquaintance would have been far too preoccupied with their own business, or listening to the sound of their own voices to have given him a second thought. But not the woman her supporters call 'the Lady.' For a short time on a stormy afternoon in Rangoon, she made him feel as if he was the only person in the room.

Those close to her admit to occasional feelings of exasperation at her willingness to give time and attention to the endless numbers of supporters and suppliants who come to her home by the lake. When I ask her about it she replies in a tone that seems almost mystified by the question. 'But every person is important. Isn't that what democracy is about, to listen to people? I am a Buddhist, this is a Buddhist country and we value human kindness and compassion,' she says.

There are frequent references to Buddhism in her conversation and in her speeches. One of her first acts upon release from house arrest was to travel out of Rangoon for a private meeting with the Sayadayaw, Burma's supreme Buddhist leader. She visits pagodas regularly and prays every day. Those who do make the pilgrimage to her slightly crumbling colonial house, with its ever-encroaching garden, find a woman who looks much younger than her fifty years. Her hair is always garlanded with jasmine, white and yellow, occasionally too a pink rose rescued from the wild green of the garden. Aung San Suu Kyi eschews make-up and jewellery apart from a pair of tiny pearl earrings and very occasionally a slender gold necklace. She wears only traditional Burmese dress: the lungi, an ankle-length wraparound cotton skirt worn by men and women alike, with blouses in darker shades of purple, green and brown. On her feet a simple pair of rubber sandals. Now and again when she rises to address the crowds who gather at her gates each weekend, she will wear yellow or white, shades of hope for those who risk harassment and arrest by attending her meetings.

The house itself is dark inside and furnished with spartan simplicity, or what one friend calls 'monastic asceticism'. It is a place of bare necessities. Wooden tables, chairs, a banquette by the sitting room window where interviews are held, and upstairs her private quarters where only she and her close aides are allowed to venture. There is also her beloved piano and one slight concession to luxury, a video player. Yet this too has an almost exclusively political purpose. It is used to watch tapes of meetings and foreign news broadcasts. Despite the relentless humidity – in summer it literally chokes the air from your lungs – there is no air conditioning. On my last visit Aung San Suu Kyi noticed rivers of perspiration running down my face in the middle of our interview. 'Wait a minute. You poor fellow. You are terribly hot,' she said, rising to switch on a solitary fan in the corner of the room. 'I don't notice it any more,' she joked.

But lack of money has also had a part to play. During the years of house arrest there was almost no money. Frequently she had to scrimp the money together to pay her electricity bill. Air conditioning and fans were non-essentials and were abandoned. Some money has now started to come in from books and donations but one senses that she is an instinctually frugal person. A handwritten note on the wall says: 'I like order and discipline. I dislike chaos and anarchy.'

'My needs are very simple and I am a great believer in simplicity. I am a vegetarian and I do not drink or smoke. Every day I get up before dawn and meditate,' she explains. 'When I want to relax I play the piano or I read, although these days there is much less time for that. Now almost all of the time is taken up with meetings with our colleagues and our people which of course is the most important thing. There is so much work to be done to get this country back on the right track.'

Aung San Suu Kyi grew up in the house by the lake and photographs of her childhood adorn the walls. They are scenes from a time before sorrow. A wide-eyed, beaming infant cradled in her parents' arms. Within months of those photo sittings, her father Bogyoke Aung San was dead, assassinated as he sat with other politicians drawing up a post-independence constitution for Burma. He is an invisible presence here, the memory which pushes his daughter forward. The photographs show the handsome young man, with a slender face and dark eyes, who led the movement for independence from Britain.

'When I was under house arrest, here on my own,' she told me, 'I would come down here at night and walk around and look up at his photograph and feel very close to him. I would say to him then: "It's you and me, Father, against them" and I felt very comforted by his presence. I felt at times as if he was there with me.'

In most of the photographs he is wearing military uniform, as befits the founder of the Burmese army. The irony of his daughter being imprisoned by the military is not lost on Aung San Suu Kyi.

'Yes, of course it seems strange, but what I would say is that the army he founded was a very different institution to the one that has taken power now in Burma. I was brought up to respect the uniform of the army, not to hate it. I want to see the army being restored to what my father believed in, an institution which protected democracy and which the people could respect and not be afraid of.'

I asked if she felt she had a destiny to lead.

'I don't know that it's my destiny to lead but it is my destiny to serve the people my father had no chance of serving to the end.'

Aung San Suu Kyi's childhood in a house dominated by politics and public service (her mother was the country's first woman ambassador) set the tone for her adult life, although she was not to become actively involved in politics until she returned from abroad in the later nineteen eighties to care for her dying mother. She travelled widely as a young woman, living with her mother in Delhi and working for the United Nations in New York for a period. As a student at Oxford where she studied politics, philosophy and economics, contemporaries remember a gentle but highly disciplined person. A friend recalls how she seemed to disapprove of the high jinks of student life. In an essay, titled 'Burmese Suu', Anne Pasternak Slater describes her as being both a genuine innocent and a person of 'fierce purity'. Her one encounter with alcohol involved a furtive sip of sherry in the ladies toilets of the Bodleian library, after which she forswore the demon drink forever; during the ritual late night discussions of boyfriends and sex, Suu would always insist that her pillow would be her only companion until she was married.

When she did get married it was to an Englishman, Michael Aris, a respected Tibetan scholar with whom she lived first in the Kingdom of Bhutan and later in Oxford. Tall, fair-haired and soft-spoken, he has always been a discreet presence in her life, a man of learning who has never been comfortable in the glare of publicity. Their two sons, Alexander and Kim, were born in the 1970s and due to her political life have spent much of their lives apart from their mother. The generals of the SLORC stripped Aung San Suu Kyi's children of their Burmese citizenship and therefore of their automatic right to enter the country. They have recently refused to grant her husband a visitor's visa. It is part of a campaign of harassment deliberately targeting her family. Among other laws introduced by the generals is one which, curiously enough, bars anyone married to a foreigner from standing for election in Burma.

She is careful to point out that many other families have suffered as well and is notably reluctant to speak about her private life beyond describing the separation as 'difficult.' However the pain of having to be an absentee mother and wife is obvious. I reminded her of Nelson Mandela's comment that what he found most difficult was the pain suffered by his family.

'I felt exactly the same way about my sons. Not so much about my husband because he was grown up and I felt he could take care of himself but my sons were very young. My youngest son was only twelve when I was first put under house arrest and I felt that very deeply. To tell the truth I tried not to think about them too much because that didn't help. I just thought they've got a good father and they will be alright. I know that, of course, is not enough but there was no point in my going around worrying and worrying about them too much.'

Her long-held conviction has been that with love and compassion relationships, however much tested by events, can survive. She also told me that she had never during her years of house arrest considered herself to be alone.

'I've never thought of loneliness as an important factor during all the years. I've never regarded myself as lonely and, in fact, I always considered myself to be quite free because I was quite free up there in my mind. They have not been able to do anything to what really mattered, to my mind, my principles. What they also did was to make me much more political. When you are on your own as a political prisoner then you tend to become so much more politicized.'

Implicit in every statement she makes, personal or political, is an absolute dedication to the ideals of freedom and justice. Burma's is a 'spiritual revolution' she says. When Aung San Suu Kyi talks about democracy it is with the kind of conviction and passion not often heard in our age. Hers is a voice that transcends the materialist scramble of modern Asia. There are constant echoes of Mahatma Gandhi and Martin Luther King.

'For me real freedom is freedom from fear,' she says. 'Unless you can live free from fear you cannot live a dignified human life. It's not possible. It's not the sort of life I want my people to live. So yes, real freedom to me is something that comes from the feeling one has inside.'

Her political philosophy has been profoundly influenced by the careers of Gandhi and Nelson Mandela. Gandhi's non-violent resistance to British rule in India has served as an example to Aung San Suu Kyi's supporters. From Mandela, she says, she has learned the virtues of perseverance and patience.

'You know I look at South Africa and say to myself "if they can achieve what they did between black and white with all their history, then surely we in Burma must be able to have justice and reconciliation too?"'

She has read every available account of the South African transition and followed the advent of majority rule on her shortwave radio, listening to the BBC as the first votes were cast in Soweto. What she is determined to do is avoid the bloodshed which marred the run-up to that election. 'I read some of the things which happened in the townships and we really must make sure that our people do not fight each other in that way,' she adds. Here her Buddhist convictions take priority. She is unwaveringly committed to the principles of non-violence. There will be no armed struggle led by Aung San Suu Kyi .

This does not however make her a weak leader or a wide-eyed, naive idealist. Dealing with the generals of the SLORC has taught her to be tough and to take nothing at face value. She has consistently refused to be either co-opted into supporting them or intimidated into giving up on the struggle for democracy. Her bottom-line demand is unwavering: the generals must respect the result of the election which gave her party more than eighty per cent of the vote in 1990. The army has a place in life that is to support democracy, she argues. There is a wonderful story she tells from the early days of her house arrest which illuminates this gritty determination.

'The day after I was placed under house arrest these military intelligence people arrived at the house with a huge bundle of paper. They had come to interrogate me of course. They wanted to ask me who my supporters were and all that kind of thing. Naturally I refused to tell them anything. And so day after day they came with the same big bundle of paper and it remained empty. In the end you know I almost felt sorry for them.' Almost but not quite. 'After a few days they were virtually pleading with me but instead I said to them that I was going to ask them questions about why they were locking up innocent people. And so I interrogated them.' By all accounts the secret policemen left with their tails between their legs.

For every day of the past seven years she has had to endure the presence of army agents in her compound. They sit just inside the gate, behind a rickety wooden table demanding the name, passport number and occupation of everybody who wants to see her. She may have been officially freed from house arrest but the harassment continues unabated. Is she not infuriated by it?

'Oh no, one gets used to it, you know. And I have a certain

amount of protection because of who I am. I don't have anything against them personally, the people at the gate. It is just what they represent that I am fighting against. We will just have to teach them the virtues of democracy. Anybody can be taught this. It's just that some people are slow learners.' Saying this, she begins to giggle mischievously. It reminds me that whenever I have met Aung San Suu Kyi I have always gone away in good humour. Little matter that most of our conversation will have been taken up with heavy political discussion.

What makes her so refreshingly different from any politician I have ever met is her capacity to laugh at the absurdities of Burma's military rulers, to joke about their attempts to demonize her, to be able to grasp the gift of hope even in her darkest moments. That and, of course, her patent sincerity.

The past year has been a steep learning curve for Aung San Suu Kyi. She has gone from the enforced solitude of the political prisoner to being the leader of a political movement struggling to find its feet again. But unlike Mandela in South Africa, her release from prison has not been accompanied by any political liberalization. If anything the repression is getting worse. People disappear into military custody. Her press officer Aye Win, a gentle and helpful man, vanished days after my last visit, picked up from his home at half past one in the morning. Torture and executions are commonplace. And yet people are still joining the National League for Democracy. Ten thousand of them gathered outside her house last weekend to catch a glimpse of 'the Lady.'

She is publicly disdainful of the cult of celebrity. Almost every answer about her own role in the struggle for democracy is prefixed by 'Of course this movement is not about individuals etc...' There is a deliberate stress on the collective nature of decision making. Ask her what she thinks of her image as a romantic heroine and she laughs. 'I always find it very strange. That is certainly not how I see myself. I always find it so strange when somebody asks me to autograph a book or something like that. I've never got used to it. I'm no different from the person I was nine years ago.'

The most dangerous days lie ahead. Rattled by the recent displays of support outside her house and the NLD's defiance of the latest clampdown, the generals of the SLORC are doubtless wondering how they might tighten the screw. Rearresting Aung San Suu Kyi would be one option, trying to silence her permanently, as they have so many of her supporters, is another. Ask her if she is worried about her personal safety and she is phlegmatic.

'No I've got out of the habit of worrying about my own security. It's not something I think about. Not because I am foolhardy or that I want to expose myself to danger. I just don't think there is any point in worrying. My life is the cause for democracy and I am linked to everybody else in that cause. There is so much to think about, I cannot just think of me.'

But do the threats, the loss of family life, the grinding daily repression not get her down? She answers without hesitation: 'What is here inside me they cannot touch. My freedom and my strength come from within and they cannot take them away. My spirit can never be taken away.'

There is one last story. For me it is the quintessential story of Aung San Suu Kyi because it speaks of courage, dignity and steely determination. Back in 1989 she and a group of supporters found themselves in a dusty town in rural Burma. The National League for Democracy had just been founded and she as general secretary was touring the country. At the time all gatherings of more than four people had been declared illegal by the regime. Aung San Suu Kyi and her followers were confronted by a line of soldiers. A captain ordered his men to level their weapons at the group and began the countdown to fire. Aung San Suu Kyi told her supporters to step to one side and she alone walked towards the guns. As the countdown was ending and the soldiers prepared to fire, an officer stepped in and countermanded the order. She remarked at the time: 'It seemed so much simpler to provide them with a single target than to bring everybody else in.' Little wonder the generals are so frightened.

Part Four

NO MAN IS AN ISLAND

NO MAN IS AN ISLAND

November 1996

Two extracts from a series of radio talks exploring the issues of
identity, ethnicity and nationalism which are so often found at
the root of conflicts around the world.

A Letter From the South

I was willing to die for Ireland. Admittedly I was five years old
at the time and, as my grandmother would point out later, I
hadn't the sense of a jackass. But it is true that for a brief period in my early childhood I was an ardent Irish nationalist,
waiting for the call to battle that would send me north across
the border, to reclaim the fourth green field and drive the
British forever from our shores.

I would lie in bed at night imagining what kind of uniform I might wear. It would have to be green of course, but
with perhaps some orange braid and a white cap to complete
the colours of the national flag. I even rounded up friends in
my Dublin neighbourhood into rival armies: I naturally led the
Irish, my younger brother or some other luckless soul would
be given command of the English and thus condemned to
eternal defeat at the hands of my glorious forces. And so we
chased around the avenues of middle Ireland avenging the
shame of our partitioned land. We must, to use one of our
most expressive Irish words, have looked like right 'eejits'.

It all began in 1966, a year English people will remember
for their victory in the World Cup but which, for this Irish
boy, was the fiftieth anniversary of the Easter Rising, when a
small group of armed nationalists rose against the British
crown and for a week fought for control of Dublin city centre.

The execution of the leaders of the Rising in the weeks afterwards turned public opinion fiercely against Britain and set the scene for the Anglo-Irish war which followed and which ended with the partition of Ireland into an independent state in the south and a British enclave in the north. The anniversary of the Rising became the focus for an outpouring of nationalist sentiment with parades, re-enactments and masses of celebration and commemoration. For weeks the country echoed to a curious blend of Te Deums and rebel ballads, 'We're off to Dublin in the green, in the green,' we sang, 'where the bayonets flash and the rifles crash to the echo of a Thompson gun.'

That was also the year I started school and, more through convenience of location than anything else, I was sent to an Irish-speaking school. It had been founded by the sisters of Patrick Pearse, the most prominent of the leaders of the Rising and a man rapidly attaining the status of sainthood in Ireland. My wife, who was in a convent school in the west of Ireland, told me she and many of her classmates fell in love with Pearse. With his dark, poetic profile and his early death by firing squad, he was the idol we had instead of pop stars. We studied his plays and poems and invoked his name in prayer. We tramped around the school yard behind a tricolour while the girls from the senior school, fierce creatures who towered over us, barked out the command, 'Ar dheis, ar chle: left right, left right.'

I remember seeing Pearse's sister, an old woman dressed entirely in black, at the commemorative mass in the school and being briefly struck by the thought that had he lived he would no longer be the handsome romantic of the photographs, but an old person shuffling along towards death. I quickly banished the thought and later, towards the end of the mass, when some poor girl's bladder gave out under the strain of waiting and a stream of urine trickled along the tiles, I was of one mind with the teachers, parents and students who harrumphed with indignation that this great celebration had been sullied by such an untimely evacuation.

That world was closed, stuffy and insular, a place in thrall to the past and its dead heroes, where our identity was not so much moulded or shaped, but drummed into us. A Catholic Ireland for a Catholic people, not merely Irish but Gaelic as well, the phrases boom down the years. Our history stressed the centuries of wrong. Famine, massacre and conquest. Plantation, betrayal and loss.

Sundays were special days for celebration of who we were, or at any rate who we thought we were. We shuffled off to mass, intoned our prayers and shuffled home to roast beef and marrowfat peas, and spent the afternoon listening to Gaelic games on the radio or playing our war-games on the lanes and streets of south Dublin. There was room for only one identity and our constitution made this abundantly clear. The Catholic church was guaranteed a unique place before the law. Our leaders regularly consulted the bishops on legislation pertaining to education and family matters. The country of my childhood was little changed from the place evoked by James Joyce who wrote of Ireland as a place where 'Christ and Caesar were fist in glove'. Back then, I had no idea that Protestants even existed and when I did learn about them, it was when a priest told me that entering a Protestant church was a sin. I could not wait to discover one and when I did, and duly entered that gallery of perdition, I waited for days for God to visit his revenge upon me. Protestants were Martians. Protestants lived in big houses and had funny accents. Protestants weren't as Irish as we were. Holy God loved Ireland and he loved good little boys who said their prayers and went to mass. What I knew about Northern Ireland and its people, Protestant and Catholic, could have been written on the back of a postage stamp. It was up there somewhere and some day we would have to get it back.

I did visit the north once on a school tour. It would have

been around 1967 and I remember very little except for the big motorway, far bigger than anything we had in the south. Also there were red postboxes and different kinds of sweets in the shops. It was not until later, as the sixties raced to a close, that the north would come exploding out of the mists of mythology and into our real lives. Our president, Eamon De Valera, a veteran of the Easter Rising who had survived to become leader of the Irish state, was an old man now, who spoke in a slow, deep voice. I saw him once when he came to our school. By then, he was stooped with age and almost completely blind. I didn't really care much for him. He was alive after all, not gloriously dead like Pearse and the others. It was his aide-de-camp's fine army uniform that caught my eye. Dev, as we called him, had been determined to ensure that a Catholic, Gaelic state would be his legacy. For a hard-headed and, on occasion, ruthless politician, he could be given to extraordinary flights of fancy when he visualized this perfect republic. It was to be a place of cosy homesteads, comely maidens and athletic youths. Sex was never mentioned. The 'deed of darkness', as one of my very Catholic relatives once called it, was designed entirely for the creation of more little Irish Catholics. Divorce and contraception were unmentionables until the late sixties. Children born out of marriage were designated illegitimate and unrecognized by the state. If a Protestant married a Catholic, they had to agree that all children of the union would be brought up as Catholics.

Now, I have no idea what it might have been like to be a Protestant growing up in this country. The fact that they only accounted for a tiny percentage of the population of the south meant that we rarely encountered them or gave them much thought. In fact, the constitution was designed less to protect us from the pernicious influence of Protestantism, than it was to make a statement about ourselves, a statement defining our difference and separateness from the big island across the water. As for the other Protestants north of the border, I had been taught in school to regard them as obstructionists who stood in the way of Irish unity. And if I tell the truth, I did not think of them very often. Our history was a history of struggles against the English and our consciousness was shaped by constant reference to those struggles.

Yet now, thirty years later, I have to say that that country is inexpressibly foreign to me. It is unrecognisable. Now when I come home on holidays I find a place that is vibrant and outward-looking, a country where identity is not a weapon or a symbol of exclusion, not something that is defined entirely by old battles and suffering, but which is willing to absorb many influences and listen to many voices. Our newspapers are full of spirited debate about the nature of Irishness. Historians, politicians and writers all argue vigorously about what our history really meant and where it is taking us. Last year we voted to remove the prohibition on divorce from our constitution. There will be those listening who feel that was a bad thing, but I choose to see it as an act of courage and generosity on the part of the Irish people. For me, it symbolized a powerful step away from a society where a specific, very Catholic view of the world was allowed to dominate the lives of three and a half million people.

There is a spirit of openness reflected in the willingness of the media to confront the most powerful figures in the land, be they churchmen or politicians, and make them truly accountable for their actions. Our president, Mary Robinson, a hugely popular figure among ordinary people, constantly urges us to embrace an Irish identity that is inclusive and willing to consider the fears of the Protestants with whom we share the island. Her message has been that our history of suffering must make us more tolerant and not less. In a year when we commemorate the death or exile of millions in the famine, an event that deeply scarred our national psyche, Mrs Robinson has been travelling the country urging people to take pride in their Irishness and not, as she put it, to feel shame because of a past that was filled with defeat and humiliation.

But what has happened to change the social and political landscape of my country? Why do I no longer feel the musty breath of the past on my back when I go home? There are many reasons for the transformation and it did not happen overnight. In retrospect, the 1960s, that time I remember as suffocating and dull, was a period of seismic change in Ireland. It may not have been obvious to us, but in numerous ways the atmosphere was being transformed. Certainly the arrival of television into nearly every home had a profound impact. Sex, once a matter for whispers and sniggers, was now openly discussed. And we entered the European Community and began shaping our school curricula to take that new multi-cultural environment into account. The decision to become enthusiastic partners in Europe signalled a move away from the economic protectionism which had impeded our development since the thirties, an abandonment of the idea that we could somehow prosper without involving ourselves in the rapidly evolving Common Market. Further afield, thousands of Irish aid workers began travelling to the Third World, coming back with perceptions broadened by their experience of working in countries just emerging from colonial rule. Our soldiers began serving on United Nations missions in the Congo, Cyprus, the Golan Heights.

In considering this new, increasingly secular Ireland, I am naturally inclined to ask whether the drift away from the certainties of our Catholic nationalist past has served to make us any less Irish? Have we sold our birthright for a mess of European subsidies and condom vending machines? Not at all. What I think is that an older Irish identity is reasserting itself. This is the voice of an Ireland whose monks and scholars travelled across early Christian Europe, who took to the seas in tiny vulnerable boats and brought their poetry, music and teaching to settlements great distances from their own island. This was an island that happily absorbed outside influence. It was only later, during the long centuries of conquest and domination that the world began to close in around us, and we began to define our identity in terms of its separateness and difference from England. Struggle and repression hardened us and for a while narrowed our vision. As W. B. Yeats memorably wrote, 'Too long a sacrifice can make a stone of the heart'.

While our vision of ourselves and what our society represented was being changed there was a darker advent in the north of this island which made it increasingly difficult to cling to the dreams and myths of the past. The explosion of violence in Northern Ireland in 1969, and the IRA and loyalist campaigns which followed, confronted us with a complex reality, one whose resolution called for something more profound than the republican slogans of the past. It simply became harder to sing the old soldiers' songs when people were dying just ninety miles to the north of us. The 'Ulster Question' is a part of our lives today as much as it was in 1922, when the island was partitioned. Yet Ulster's bitter words and deeds seem strangely out of step with the new Ireland you have heard me describing . The difference is that in the south, whatever our political or religious viewpoints, we share a vision of ourselves as Irish. We have grown secure in our identity and in that process the banging of the green drum, the preaching of nationalist pieties has become far less important. In the north there is, for both nationalist and loyalist, no similar sense of security. Both feel their right to self-determination is either being ignored or threatened and on both sides there are men willing to kill and die for the sake of identity. For many southerners, the bitterness of this struggle seems incomprehensible. The temptation for many is to turn away or to wish that somebody would build a large fence along the border and keep them all, loyalist and nationalist, inside. That is an attitude of mind which we must avoid if there is to be any hope of resolving the conflict. We cannot embrace Europe and the wider world and ignore the north, however fractious its politics.

This preoccupation with Ireland has stayed with me, perhaps even grown more intense during my reporting on ethnic struggles elsewhere in the world. Through South Africa, Rwanda, in the jungles of Sri Lanka I have heard the echoes of our old quarrel come back across the years. And I know that while men still kill in the name of Irishness and Britishness less than a hundred miles from my home, I will find it difficult to speak of a truly new Ireland.

A Letter from Africa

Below the village of Rusomo, the River Kagera flows into a steep ravine that forms the natural border between Tanzania and Rwanda. There is a small waterfall where the river narrows before entering the gorge. In the rainy season the river swells and thickens with brown upland silt. As it sweeps down from the highlands, it gathers into its currents huge clumps of elephant grass and numerous small trees. These are then swept and tossed across the Rusomo Falls before settling into the calmer waters on the Tanzanian side.

In the late spring of 1994, it was much the same story with human corpses. They too twisted and turned, rose and dropped and came bouncing over the falls before they found the still water which would carry them slowly down to Lake Victoria. Of course at first they did not look dead to me. They looked like swimmers ... because the strong currents invested them with powers of movement that seemed, temporarily, to deny the fact of their mortality. In fact so lifelike did they appear that for a few moments I winced as I watched them thrown against the rocks, imagining the pain they must be feeling. It was only beyond the falls, where they floated lifeless among the trees and grass, that one could accept the certainty of death. I watched this from the bridge. The border guards told me people had been floating through in their hundreds, every day for weeks. Many had their hands tied behind their backs. They had been shot, hacked, clubbed, burned, drowned. The genocide of the Tutsis had been progressing at a fearsome rate for more than a month. By the time it would finish, up to a million people would be dead. Consider the mathematics of this horror: in one hundred days, one million people. The area around Rusomo had recently been captured by the Tutsi-dominated Rwandan Patriotic Front (RPF). While the world dithered, this guerrilla army had launched an all-out attack on the Hutu government forces responsible for the genocide. Now they were steadily advancing, driving thousands of government troops and Hutu refugees before them. In the days before the RPF arrived at Rusomo, a quarter of a million refugees had fled across the bridge. They would, of course, have seen the bodies floating past and many among these refugees would have taken some part in the slaughter. For this genocide was a crime of mass complicity, a neighbourly slaughter in which killer and victim invariably knew each other. Just before the bridge lay a huge pile of machetes and axes, dumped there as the refugees escaped towards Tanzania. Many of these weapons were stained with blood.

I leaned over the bridge and noticed that two bodies had become lodged in the rocks at the side of the gorge. One was that of a man. The other that of a baby, between six and twelve months old. I saw that the child had been killed with a machete, a gash across its skull. It did not seem like a real child. It looked like a doll. Or perhaps it might be more truthful to say I did not want to accept that it was a child. It was easier for my eyes to tell me that it was made of plastic. I looked again and of course knew that further back along the river, perhaps fifty to one hundred miles further back, an adult had taken a knife and ended the life of this child and then hurled it into the water. I stepped back from the bridge and felt like being sick. Closing my eyes I could hear the sound of the water rushing through the gorge and, beyond us in Tanzania, the noise of cattle being herded through the savannah grasslands. They were normal sounds and they helped me to control the urge to retch. I kept my eyes closed and gripping the rails of the bridge made my way back to our car in the manner of a blind man. I did not want to look back at the river, to see it ever again. And on the journey north to Kigali where the war still raged, I kept asking myself the same question: 'What kind of man would kill a baby? What kind of man?'

Genocide is the word we use to describe what happens when one group turns on another and seeks to destroy it. And in the case of Africa we almost invariably explain such a slaughter as a matter of tribalism. A crazy African thing. A horror somehow mitigated by the knowledge that Africans have always been prone to this kind of behaviour. Genocide prompted by implacable and ancient tribal antagonisms. Yet, it is my belief that Rwanda offers a profound challenge to this analysis. Scratch below the surface of this genocide and you will find not a simple issue of tribal hatreds but a complex web of politics, economics, history, psychology and a struggle for identity. This was not something I realized when I was despatched to Rwanda two years ago. Like many of my colleagues, I drove in from Uganda believing that the short stocky ones had simply decided to turn on the tall thin ones because that was the way it had always been. Yet now, two years later, when I ask the question: 'What kind of man ...' I think the answer is very different. What kind of man? Anyone, anyone at all. A man like you or me. Not a psychopath. Not a natural born killer. A man born without prejudice or hatred. But rather a man who was conditioned by the preachings of powerful men.

Men who said that the survival of the Hutus depended on the death of small Tutsi children, who said: 'Don't repeat the mistake of '59. Kill the children.' For little Tutsis grow into adult Tutsis and they planned to make eternal slaves of the Hutus. 'Kill the children and save your race,' said the powerful ones. In 1959, when the Tutsi aristocracy had been overthrown, thousands had been killed and thousands more driven into exile. Among the many who fled the country were children. And it was they who now formed the backbone of the Rwandan Patriotic Front which was fighting against the genocidal regime.

What happened in Rwanda was the result of cynical manipulation by powerful political and military leaders. Faced with the choice of sharing some of their wealth and power with the Rwandan Patriotic Front, they chose to vilify that organization's main support group, the Tutsis. The authorities told the impoverished Hutu peasantry that the Tutsis planned to take their land. They summoned up memories of the colonial days when the Tutsis overlordship had guaranteed second-class citizenship for the Hutus. Remember your shame. Remember how they humiliated us. Be proud of your Hutu blood, they told the peasants. Intellectuals were recruited into the cause of creating a pan-Hutu consciousness. University professors, churchmen, journalists – all travelled the country disseminating the propaganda of hate. The Tutsis were characterized as vermin. *Inyenzi in kinyarwanda* – cockroaches who should be stamped on without mercy. Mercy was a sign of weakness. Show them any mercy and they will make slaves of you again. You will be humiliated and shamed once again. There were powerful echoes of Hitler's Germany and the demonization of the Jews. In much the same way as the Nazis exploited latent anti-semitism in Germany, so did the forces of Hutu extremism identify and whip into murderous frenzy the historical sense of grievance against the Tutsis. In colonial

Rwanda and Burundi the German and later Belgian rulers cultivated the notion that the Tutsis were somehow less African, more European and, by extension, superior to their Hutu fellow countrymen. They ruled through and with the assistance of a Tutsi elite built around a king and a group of land-owning clans. In justifying this form of colonial and minority rule the Belgians resorted to all manner of racial nonsense. They cited the tallness of the Tutsis, their aquiline facial features, the fact that they preferred to raise cattle than till the land as evidence of a superior civilization. Consider the words of one Belgian doctor writing of the differences between Hutus and Tutsis:

> 'The latter ... have a distant, reserved, courteous and elegant manner ... The rest of the population is Bantu, the Bahutu. They are Negroes with all the Negroid characteristics ... they are childish in nature, both timid and lazy and, as often as not, extremely dirty.'

All manner of humiliating folly was employed in the name of proving this theory of innate Tutsi superiority. Skulls and noses were measured. Legends were invented to explain the presence of these superior beings in the centre of Africa. The favoured notion was that the Tutsis had come down from Ethiopia. Even the respected American writer John Gunther fell for this utterly unsubstantiated myth. In 1954 he wrote of the Tutsis:

> 'They are not Negroes though they may be jet black. A Hamitic or Nilotic people, they are pastoral nomads and cattlemen who came down from the north, and they startlingly resemble Ethiopians ... they are proud, sophisticated and not particularly energetic. Several times we saw Watutsi lords sitting on bicycles being pushed by their vassals ... tallness is a symbol of racial exclusiveness and pure blood.'

Another Belgian colonial tract described the Tutsis as:

'*Tall and noble and regarded as demi-gods by the Hutus who were themselves creatures with souls, sad and passive, with never a thought for the morrow.*'

It is important to remember that all of this was done less because the Belgians had any real desire to embrace the Tutsis as their equals, but rather because they needed the Tutsis as their allies to maintain a fundamentally unjust political dispensation. In other words, race and identity were used as a means to create and preserve an inherently unjust power structure. The effect of this injustice and of the stereotyping of Hutus as lesser beings was to create murderous feelings of inferiority and resentment among the majority. When, at the end of the fifties, the Belgians relinquished power, the Hutus rose up and began the first of many campaigns of massacre against their former Tutsi rulers. The Belgians, of course, escaped back to Belgium. The eruption of violence which seemed to the world like a simple matter of tribal hatred had its roots in the politics of power and privilege.

By the time the 1990s arrived a small group of Hutus had created their own corrupt aristocracy, built around the former army chief Juvenal Habyarimana and a clique of his supporters from northern Rwanda. This dictatorship kept the lion's share of wealth while ordinary Hutus struggled along at subsistence level. The Tutsis were a cowed minority, discriminated against in every sphere of life but left largely unmolested because they no longer represented a political threat. And then the Rwandan Patriotic Front suddenly appeared, sweeping into Rwanda from their bases in exile in Uganda. These children of Tutsis, driven out in 1959, had come back to claim a share of power. The reaction among Habyarimana and his supporters was one of barely concealed panic. They called in French military support and without this would have been defeated by the RPF in 1990. Worse still, Habyarimana now faced growing calls for democratization from moderate Hutu groups, tired of his corrupt and authoritarian rule. There is strong evidence to suggest that Habyarimana feared losing power to the moderates. Threatened from within and outside, Habyarimana and his northern Hutu clique seized on the one element guaranteed to mobilize public support behind the government: hatred of the Tutsis.

Thus newspapers and radio stations began to exhort the people to rally behind Hutuism. Drive the Tutsis out and show them no mercy, the virulent Radio Mille Collines demanded. A Hutu militia was established, the Interahamwe: those who stand together. The people were being conditioned for a final solution that would rid Rwanda of all political opposition to the government – all of the Tutsis and the moderate Hutus who opposed the regime. Again, remember, this was not about tribalism first and foremost but about preserving the concentration of wealth and power in the hands of the elite. The Tutsis were convenient scapegoats and the more moderate Hutus could easily be condemned as traitors to their tribe. When Habyarimana himself seemed to weaken under international pressure and consider power-sharing, his jet was blown out of the sky. Much as the burning of the Reichstag provided Hitler with a pretext for taking power, the murder of Habyarimana, very probably by his associates, gave the signal for the onset of Rwanda's final solution. On the evening of 6 April 1994, the killing began.

And so I ask of you to think of that night and the silence at first, then followed by the sound of gunfire. Then the roadblocks appearing everywhere. And the soldiers and militiamen going from house to house to house. The dead piling up in the streets. Corpses falling one onto the other in the swift calamity of blood. And think of the fear as a Tutsi walks up to one of these roadblocks because he is trying to get home and off the streets. There are men with machetes and axes and they are drunk. They seize his card and notice immediately that he is a Tutsi. A UN soldier standing on a balcony nearby sees what happens next. The man is knocked to the ground with a punch. He is pulled to his feet and every man at the roadblock takes turns to strike him. The man is crying and pleading for his life. From a distance it is hard to tell what he is saying. It could be that he is telling them that his wife and children are waiting at home. At any rate they do not listen except to laugh and then punch and kick him again. One of them raises a machete and strikes the man on the shoulder. He falls to the ground, still pleading. But he is a Tutsi, a hated one and deserving of no mercy. The UN soldier calls out. His name is Emmanuel Quist and he comes from Ghana. A big good-humoured man, he has served with the UN in several countries. But this hatred is unlike anything he has seen before. The killers look up and notice him and for a moment they stop. The man on the ground must think he has a hope. But the gang drag him down a laneway. From his balcony, Emmanuel Quist is shouting himself hoarse but he can see machetes rising and falling in the laneway. The men return to the roadblock and the process is repeated. Emmanuel Quist is under orders not to intervene. The UN has no mandate to intervene. The killing goes on.

Later in Kigali, as the siege thunders around us, a French priest tells me that he wonders if he is going mad because of the things he has seen. 'They think that by killing the other ethnic groups they can solve all their problems,' he says. In this madhouse every man has his private torment. The priest has had to leave a group of Tutsi orphans behind in government territory. His colleague was wounded and they simply had no choice other than to escape. But the priest cannot forget the children's voices. They begged him to lock them in a room at the back of the church. The oldest of the children thought the militia might not search that room. And now the priest is telling me how he turned the key and listened to those small frightened voices growing ever more faint as he walked away. I think he believes the children are dead and he is probably correct. 'Rwanda,' he says and there are tears in his eyes. Rwanda. And so I think to myself yet again. What kind of man can kill a child? A man not born to hate but who has learned hatred. A man like you or me.

INDEX

INDEX

INDEX